NEWPORT

D1571218

NEWPORT

A Concise History

NEWPORT HISTORICAL SOCIETY

*Revised by the staff of the Newport Historical Society
and edited by Elizabeth C. Stevens*

THE
History
PRESS

Published by The History Press
Charleston, SC
www.historypress.com

First published 2024

Manufactured in the United States

ISBN 9781467155472

Library of Congress Control Number: 2024931891

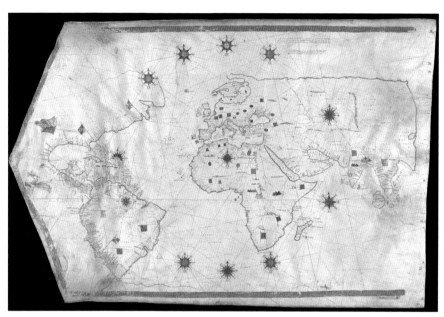

Girolamo da Verrazzano mapped the lands his brother, Florentine navigator Giovanni da Verrazzano, encountered when he crossed the Atlantic between 1523 and 1528. In service to King Francis I of France, Girolamo included French standards to designate the region as Nova Gallia (New Gaul); the map shows "Refugio" (purportedly Newport Harbor), where Verrazzano's ship *Delfina* anchored for fifteen days in 1524. *G201:1/15, National Maritime Museum, Greenwich, England.*

Contents

FOREWORD

S ince its founding in 1854, the Newport Historical Society has been dedicated to telling the story of Newport County. Traditional histories of Newport focused on the founding of the town by religious dissidents and their contributions to religious freedom. There is no denying that the town's first settlers' agreement to support liberty of conscience, a revolutionary idea that was codified in the Colony of Rhode Island's Charter of 1663, was a pivotal moment that paved the way for other key moments in Newport's history—the American Revolution, the Gilded Age and beyond. However, this traditional narrative omits a great deal, particularly the histories of people of Native American and African descent. And while it is well known that Newport was a thriving colonial seaport, it is less often acknowledged that this prosperity was in large part due to Newport's dominant role in the transatlantic slave trade. This edition of *Newport: A Concise History*, with the aid of new scholarship, aims to tell a more inclusive history of Newport that begins with the area's first inhabitants and includes the contributions of the people who were brought here in captivity and those of later groups of immigrants who worked to build the physical city and diverse community that still exists today. Telling hundreds of years of history in a concise manner is a difficult task; for the sake of brevity, there are aspects of Newport's story that have been abbreviated or left out altogether. However, as each new wave of scholars uncovers more of the complex history of this city, the Newport Historical Society will continue to bring that history to you.

Ingrid Peters
Deputy Director for Operations and Academic Services,
Newport Historical Society

PREFACE TO THE PRESENT AND PREVIOUS EDITIONS

Newport: A Concise History is a revision of an earlier version of the same title that was published in 2008. The latter, in turn, was an extensive revision of *Newport: A Short History*, a book that appeared in 1992 that was a reworking of *Newport, 1639–1976: An Historical Sketch*, published in 1976 by the late C.P.B. Jefferys.

In 1976, C.P.B. Jefferys, the then-president of the Newport Historical Society who taught history at nearby St. George's School, wrote an introduction for Florence Simister's book *Streets of the City*, in which he divided Newport's three-and-a-half centuries into six periods. Both the book for which it was written and the introduction itself proved to be so popular that Jefferys was persuaded by friends and associates at the Newport Historical Society to expand his thoughts into a short history of Newport. He framed the resulting *Newport, 1639–1976: An Historical Sketch* with an eye to entertain as well as inform.

As Jefferys made clear in the preface to the 1976 edition, the book was not a "scholarly treatise," and this revision is aimed at continuing the general tone Jefferys himself took, while including updated scholarship and expanding on areas that previous editions treated only in passing.

The current iteration of *Newport: A Concise History* draws on the work of a number of historians and scholars. We would like to especially acknowledge the contributions of David J. Silverman, for his permission to adapt his essay "Native Americans on the Land in Rhode Island and the Arrival of the English," first published in John Tschirch's *Newport: The Artful City* (Newport

Historical Society, 2020), and John Quinn, who shared his knowledge about the Irish community in Newport. In his lectures and writings, Keith Stokes has illuminated the history of Newport's thriving Black community. Christian McBurney's collection of articles in his *World War II Rhode Island* (The History Press, 2017) and Robert B. MacKay's *The Golden Age of Newport Yachting Between the Wars* (The History Press, 2021) were helpful in adding information to this new edition. "A Town-By-Town Review of the hurricane of 1938 in Rhode Island," by the Federal Writers Project, as reproduced on the website smallstatebighistory.com, enhanced our description of the Hurricane of 1938 in Newport. We are also grateful for the research and writing of *Newport History* authors John Rice, Joey La Neve DeFrancesco, Robert Cvornyek, Christopher Magra and William P. Leeman and his Salve Regina University students Brittany Fox and Ellen E. Tuttle. We would like to acknowledge the expertise of Nancy Whipple Grinnell, curator emerita of the Newport Art Museum, who contributed insights and information about the museum and the nineteenth-century Newport art community, and art historian Ron Onorato for clarifying architectural terms.

Other contributors to this edition include Kaela Bleho, Bert Lippincott, Bridget Newton, Sean O'Brien, Ingrid Peters, Elizbeth C. Stevens and Ruth Taylor. Credit is also due to those who worked on previous editions of this book, including Barbara Lloyd Baker, Jane Carey, Evelyn Cherpak, Theodore Gatchel, John Hattendorf, Curtis LaFrance and Sue Maden.

1

EARLIEST INHABITANTS

INDIGENOUS PEOPLES

The history of Newport begins with its Indigenous peoples. While the town as we know it was founded in 1639 by English immigrants, Indigenous peoples stewarded and cultivated the region for thousands of years. Their centrality to the history of Newport and Rhode Island has long been overlooked.

The earliest inhabitants of Aquidneck Island were Indigenous peoples who had inhabited southern New England for at least twelve thousand years before the arrival of European explorers and immigrants. In the Algonquian language, used by the Narragansett people who first lived here, the name *Aquidneck* is said to mean "on the island," later romanticized by Victorian-era writers as "Isle of Peace." The well-watered landscape of bays, inlets, rivers, ponds and marshes on and around the island supported a bevy of wild foods to sustain human populations. There was a stunning variety of salt- and freshwater fish, waterfowl and shellfish. To take advantage of such resources, people crafted dugout canoes called mishoon (plural: mishoonash), sometimes capable of carrying dozens of men and navigating miles out to sea. The discovery of heaps of discarded shells from 80–220 CE (current era) on the island provides ample archaeological evidence of the diets of Indigenous peoples who lived and worked here for thousands of years.

Beginning in the early Archaic period, 8000–6000 BCE (before the current era), Indigenous peoples in the area began to follow a seasonal

Giovanni da Verrazzano explored the East Coast of North America between 1523 and 1528. In a 1524 letter to King Francis I, he wrote in great detail about the peoples he encountered along what is now the New England coast. *Image ID 5198126, The New York Public Library Digital Collections.*

round in which they spent spring at the riverside fish runs, summer along the shoreline and fall and winter inland to hunt terrestrial animals. By at least the late Archaic period (3000–1000 BCE), there were several seasonal habitations on Aquidneck Island, evident in the archaeological sites preserved underneath Newport's Great Friends Meeting House. Other archaeological sites on nearby Conanicut Island (also known as Jamestown) show evidence of human occupation from 2500 BCE, such as the remains of house frames,

A replica of a wetu, a circular dwelling used by the Indigenous peoples of Rhode Island. *The Haffenreffer Museum of Anthropology, Brown University.*

hearths, trash pits and tools. Conanicut Island also has an ancient cemetery with remains dating to 1280 BCE. Native peoples' proprietorship and stewardship of the region is evident in both the archaeological record and in Indigenous oral histories.

Developments in material culture and technologies, such as the arrival of the bow and arrow and of maize and bean cultivation, reflect an interconnectedness across vast regions. The bow and arrow, which came from Arctic Indigenous peoples, was a vast improvement over the spear in terms of range and portability. The cultivation of maize and beans began in Mexico and spread through what is now the southwestern United States and eventually into New England. The expansion of maize cultivation was a stunning feat of human engineering in which cultivators—certainly women, given their responsibility for the crop—bred ever larger cobs and selected seeds that could grow in colder, wetter environments.

Southern New England was the last place in America to which maize spread. Adding horticultural produce to wild foods enabled Indigenous peoples in southern New England, particularly along Narragansett Bay, to sustain populations as dense as those found anywhere in Native America. The overall population for southern New England circa 1600 CE was between 126,000 and 144,000, with the Wampanoags on the east side of

Narragansett Bay boasting an estimated population of 21,000 to 24,000 and the Narragansetts on the west side some 30,000. It would take European colonists in southern New England over a century before their numbers reached the collective heights of these groups.

When the English began settling in Narragansett Bay in the mid- to late 1630s, the political relations of Indigenous peoples along Narragansett Bay were in flux. The primary Wampanoag sachem Ousamequin (or Massasoit) lived in the village of Sowams at the head of the Mount Hope Peninsula, where the Taunton River empties into the east side of Narragansett Bay, a stone's throw north of what became the town of Portsmouth on Aquidneck Island. Not long before, Ousamequin's people had occupied the head of Narragansett Bay, where the city of Providence is now located, as well as Aquidneck, and battled with the

Stone knife recovered in Rhode Island, circa 1000 BCE. *RHIX173882A, Rhode Island Historical Society.*

Narragansetts for territory and tributaries on the west bank. By the time the English arrived on the scene, the Narragansetts had driven the Wampanoags east of the Providence and Seekonk Rivers.

There are several possible explanations for the rivalry of the Wampanoags and the Narragansetts. One is that the Wampanoags fought for control of the planting grounds of Narragansett Bay, which were among the richest in the region. The explorer Giovanni da Verrazzano visited the bay in 1524, becoming the first European to record a venture to the area that is now known as southern New England. As recorded in remarks published in *The Voyages of Giovanni da Verrazzano, 1524–1528* (1970), the explorer noted that its "fields extend for 25 to 30 leagues; they are open and free of any obstacles or trees, and so fertile that any kind of seed would produce excellent crops." Some of the earliest archaeological evidence for horticulture among southern New England Indigenous peoples comes from Narragansett Bay. There was also competition between the tribes to acquire quahog shells and the labor to produce shell beads for the Mohawk tribes of what is now New York State.

A third point of contention between the two tribes would have been access to European trading vessels, which began to appear intermittently as early as 1524. Indigenous peoples sought the Europeans' metal tools and implements, brightly colored cloth, mirrors, glass beads and other jewelry.

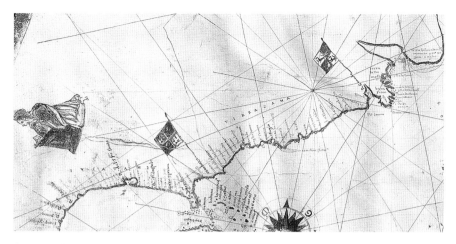

Detail of Girolamo da Verrazzano's map of North America (circa 1540) showing what is now the Rhode Island coast. Giovanni da Verrazzano visited Narragansett Bay in 1524. *G201:1/15, National Maritime Museum, Greenwich, England.*

They especially prized European copper goods. For sachems of a densely populated horticultural region trying to consolidate and extend their followings against competitors, securing a new source of exotic luxury goods with which they could reward their supporters was a potential boon.

Whatever the source of the Wampanoag-Narragansett dispute, the advantage went to the Narragansetts after an unidentified European epidemic disease devastated the Wampanoags from 1616 to 1619, more than halving their population and wiping out some villages entirely. The Narragansetts escaped the disaster, apparently because of their limited contact with infected Wampanoags. The Narragansetts used this newfound advantage to force the Wampanoags from the head of Narragansett Bay and the islands, including Aquidneck.

The Wampanoag-Narragansett rivalry was the backdrop to the first decades of English colonization on Narragansett Bay. When Roger Williams fled Massachusetts in the winter of 1636, he first sought refuge with Ousamequin, who offered him a site east of the Seekonk River at the head of the bay. Later, Williams was forced to relocate just a few miles west to an area at the confluence of the Moshassuck and Woonasquatucket Rivers, the intermediate zone between the Wampanoags and the Narragansetts, in a place he called Providence. Both Ousamequin and Canonicus, the Narragansetts' sachem, supported this move. Williams became a go-between and scribe for these Indigenous leaders in their relations with other tribes and colonies.

Above: A mishoon, or Indigenous dugout canoe, is crafted by lighting controlled fires inside a log before carving out the interior. This watercraft was common throughout North America by the seventeenth century; the traditions of crafting mishoonash are maintained today. *Plimoth Patuxet Museums.*

Right: Roger Williams, engraved in 1847 by Frederick Halpin. *Image ID 424056, the New York Public Library.*

Opposite: A portrait of Wampanoag sachem Metacom, also known as King Philip (circa 1860). *The Haffenreffer Museum of Anthropology, Brown University.*

Roger Williams

Over the next decade, Ousamequin granted Roger Williams and other Rhode Island colonists the right to settle and use tracts all around the northern and eastern edges of Narragansett Bay and its islands, including Aquidneck, within the Wampanoag-Narragansett no man's land. The Narragansetts did the same, ceding land north of their core territory, which the Wampanoags contested.

To be sure, the English compensated the sachems for these grants—for instance, paying Ousamequin five fathoms of Wampum for the right to graze livestock in what became the town of Portsmouth. However, Williams knew that these sums were merely one aspect of what the sachems expected in return. They wanted the English as friends to advise their people in politics, defend them in times of danger and treat them with respect and hospitality.

Indigenous power along Narragansett Bay was such that early English immigrants generally adhered to Indigenous expectations about joint use of the land and satisfied Wampanoag and Narragansett complaints about violations, if out of self-preservation rather than moral principle. As late as the 1660s, the total population of colonial Rhode Island was still only about 1,500, or about one-tenth the size of the population of the Narragansetts, so at this time, the colonists in Rhode Island would have been respectful in their dealings with their Indigenous neighbors. Regionally, the English had a greater advantage, and they used it to expand their land, jurisdiction and religion at the expense of Indigenous peoples in colonies like Massachusetts, Plymouth and eventually, Rhode Island.

The result was King Philip's War of 1675–76, in which the allied Wampanoags, Narragansetts, Nipmucs and other Indigenous peoples initially devastated English towns throughout the Northeast, only to be defeated within the year at the hands of the colonists and their coalition of Indigenous allies. It took that war for the English to seize control of the region, including Aquidneck, by killing and enslaving thousands of Indigenous people and seizing their territory. Even then, there remained small communities of Narragansett and Wampanoag survivors who still considered Aquidneck an Indigenous place with a deep Indigenous history.

European Exploration and the Naming of Rhode Island

A number of explorers sailed into or past Narragansett Bay long before the first English settlers arrived. Europeans are thought to have first encountered Aquidneck Island during explorations of the sixteenth century. Italian explorer Giovanni da Verrazzano sailed for the king of France between 1524 and 1528 on the first recorded and documented voyage to explore the coast of North America from Florida to Newfoundland. In a letter to King Francis I, detailing his journey, Verrazzano spoke of Block Island being

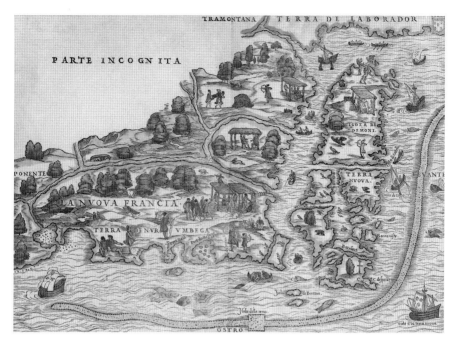

A woodcut map of "New France," by Giacomo Gastaldi, 1556, based largely on the voyages of Jacques Cartier and Giovanni da Verrazzano, showing "Port du Refuge," likely Narragansett Bay. *G 3435 1556 R3 c.2 MAP, Centre for Newfoundland Studies, Memorial University of Newfoundland.*

about the size of the Island of Rhodes in the southeastern Aegean Sea. He probably anchored in what is now Newport Harbor for fifteen days in 1524, calling the place "Refugio."

Roger Williams, the founder of the town of Providence, read a translation of Verrazzano's account in Richard Hakluyt's *Divers Voyages* (1582) and mistakenly thought Verrazzano was referring to Aquidneck Island rather than Block Island. In 1637, Williams named Aquidneck Island "Ile of Rhods or Rhod-Island," and in 1644, a court of election for Newport and Portsmouth confirmed Williams's choice as the official name for the island. A century later, in 1743, the third town on the island, Middletown (the first being Portsmouth, settled in 1638), seceded from Newport and received a town charter of its own. In 1663, King Charles II's charter joined Rhode Island with Providence, and the official name of the colony, then the state, became Rhode Island and Providence Plantations. (The name of the state reverted back to simply "Rhode Island" after a referendum in 2020.) In addition to Verrazzano, other early European explorers also included the Dutchman Adrien Bloeck, for whom Block Island was ultimately named.

2

Seventeenth Century

Newport Begins, 1639–1700

The first English settlers who arrived on Aquidneck Island in 1638 were Anne Hutchinson and her followers who had been banished from Boston for their unorthodox religious beliefs. In the mid-1630s, a religious furor swept through the Massachusetts Bay Colony. The Antinomian Controversy (*Antinomian* means "against the law") was an outgrowth of theological divisions between leaders of the strictly Puritan communities and more radically dissenting inhabitants who believed that religious salvation was a matter of faith and divine grace rather than a condition of living a "godly" life. The arguments, which became political as well as religious, resulted in the entrenchment of the Puritan view in both society and law within Massachusetts and the banishment of many of the leaders and adherents of opposing sects.

Anne Hutchinson was a leading Antinomian; many of her supporters followed her into exile on Aquidneck Island. The group worked with Roger Williams, who was previously banished from Massachusetts for religious dissent and was the founder of Providence, Rhode Island, in 1637, to negotiate the purchase of settlement rights from Canonicus and Miantonomi, sachems of the Narragansett tribe. The agreement, signed by both the colonists and Indigenous people, stated that the current inhabitants would remove themselves from the island. There is abundant evidence, however, that Indigenous people did not entirely abandon Aquidneck Island but

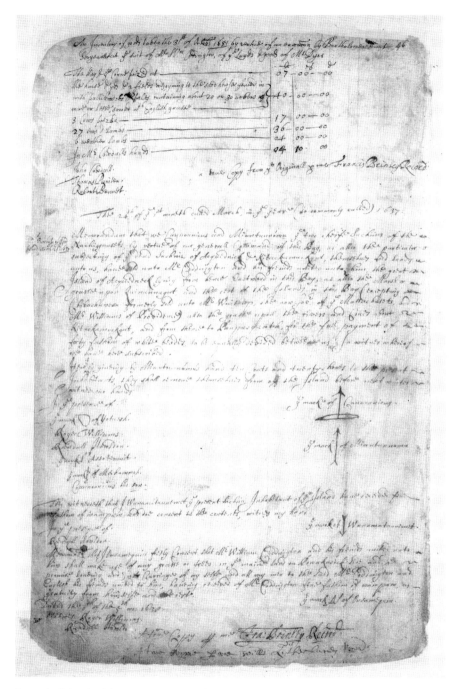

Record of the deed for Aquidneck Island, 1637. The deed features the marks of Canonicus and Miantonomi, sachems of the Narragansett tribe. *The Rhode Island State Archives.*

rather continued to make use of this land while finding ways to adapt to the presence of European settlements. The small group of religious dissidents led by Anne Hutchinson settled first on the northern tip of Aquidneck Island near the area known as Common Fence Point, now part of Portsmouth. The English colonists named the settlement "Pocasset" after the local Algonquian language name for the site.

Almost from the beginning, religious disagreements divided this first settlement. In 1639, a splinter group led by Nicholas Easton, William Coddington and Dr. John Clarke moved to the southern tip of Aquidneck Island, where, by a deep-water harbor and freshwater spring, they established the town of Newport.

Religious Toleration

The formal origin of Newport can be traced to April 28, 1639, when the Newport Compact was signed by William Coddington, William Dyer, Nicholas Easton, John Coggeshall, William Brenton, Henry Bull, Jeremy Clarke, Thomas Hazard and Dr. John Clarke, who was instrumental in convincing the early settlers to commit to a practice of religious liberty. This document, along with similar ones signed in Providence in 1636 and Portsmouth in 1638, outlined a shift from the standard form of most English colonial settlements. While many of the earliest settlers of Newport became Baptists, there was to be no formal established church around which the town would coalesce. Instead, freedom of conscience was to be the rule. Word of a town founded on the basis of liberty of conscience and religion quickly spread, and other religious groups seeking sanctuary from the banishment and persecution they suffered elsewhere began to arrive.

By 1658, a Jewish community had immigrated to Newport from the Island of Curaçao in the Caribbean. The group was made up mostly of Sephardic Jews who had been forced to flee Portugal and Spain. Word of Newport's toleration spread, and soon, a number of Jewish families arrived in the young town. Led by Moses Pacheco and Mordecai Campenall, they purchased land for a cemetery, established homes and obtained the unprecedented freedom to practice their religion openly. This marks one of the first instances of acceptance of a Jewish population in a western colony. However, the acceptance was not total, as Jews, even property owners, were not formally permitted to vote in civic elections—though they would come

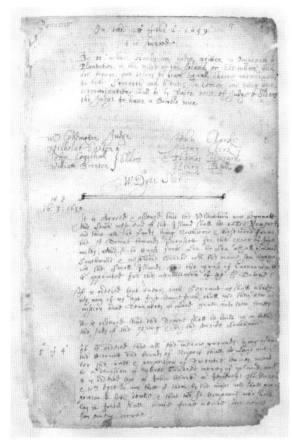

Left: Newport Compact, 1739. *The Rhode Island State Archives.*

Below: The Great Friends Meeting House (shown here circa 1857) was constructed on the northeast corner of the Great Common in 1699—the original settlement that evolved over time into Washington Square and its side streets. The building was enlarged repeatedly over the next two centuries. *2004.13.216, Collection of the Newport Historical Society.*

to possess a great deal of civic and political authority—until the end of the eighteenth century.

Members of a Protestant Christian sect known as Quakers also arrived in Newport in 1657. The Society of Friends, as they were officially called, held egalitarian beliefs that put them at odds with both the established Church of England, as well the Puritan churches in North America. Having been expelled from New Amsterdam (now New York City) to the south, as well as Massachusetts Bay to the north, the Quakers found a haven in Newport. The Quaker ideals of hard work, simplicity of living and public and private virtue meant that they not only assimilated quickly but, in a very short time, also became extremely influential in the civic and political life of the town.

During the seventeenth century, the growing town came to include many marginalized and persecuted religious groups. By the early eighteenth century, Anglicans, Baptists, Congregationalists, Jews, Seventh Day Baptists, Quakers and other groups dwelt together in Newport in reasonable harmony. While one observer described the village as "a receptacle for people of several sorts of opinions," Cotton Mather, a leading Puritan clergyman in Massachusetts, characterized the settlement as a "sewer," because people of all religious faiths were welcome in the town.

ESTABLISHING A GOVERNMENT

Newport and Rhode Island at large found it possible to engage in this early form of religious and political liberty due to the unique political structure of the colony. Rhode Island did not have an appointed royal governor. Although many of the political institutions in local government were derived from British law, custom and tradition, the Rhode Island colony was singular in that it was a virtual democracy, where freemen (those who met the land qualification for voting privileges) were allowed to vote on local matters in a town meeting. Notably, this privilege did not include Jewish men, Indigenous men, men of African descent or women. By the standards of the day, however, this was a remarkably enlightened form of government, and considerable authority was retained by those individuals who were considered citizens.

Despite its non-Puritan establishment, Rhode Island's civic leaders maintained cordial relationships with dissenting leaders in England.

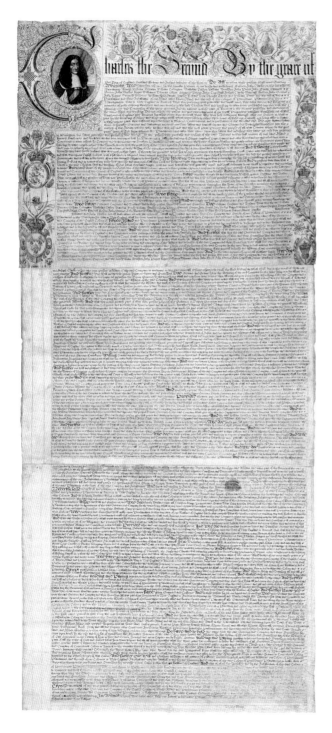

Rhode Island's 1663 royal charter. *The Rhode Island State Archives.*

This would prove beneficial in 1644, when England was in the throes of civil war. Thanks to the efforts of Roger Williams and his connections to Puritan leaders in England, a commission of Parliament granted a patent to Newport, Portsmouth and Providence, thereby creating the colony of Rhode Island and Providence Plantations and legally codifying many of the founding principles of Newport and surrounding communities. Despite what seemed to be a unifying political movement, the different towns around Narragansett Bay considered themselves independent of each other. On Aquidneck Island, William Coddington, one of the original settlers of Newport, had himself named president of the colony for life in 1651. This act was not well received. Delegations were dispatched back to England to debate the issue. Oliver Cromwell and the Council of State revoked Coddington's authority in 1652, but with the restoration of the monarchy in May 1660, all the acts of the commonwealth were rescinded, including Rhode Island's 1644 charter.

With a new legal basis for the colony now required, Dr. John Clarke of Newport, a founder of the town and the colony's agent in London, began to work for a new charter. On July 8, 1663, King Charles II granted a new and very liberal charter to the English Colony of Rhode Island that guaranteed self-government and established "a lively experiment…with full liberty in religious concernments." This charter was the first in western history to go beyond toleration and to make religious liberty a principle of corporate existence. It remained the constitution of the colony and, later, the State of Rhode Island and Providence Plantations for 179 years until it was finally superseded in 1843.

Aside from establishing religious toleration in the colony, the Charter of 1663 also established a general assembly under an elected (rather than appointed) governor. Each town in the colony was to have a duly appointed number of assemblymen chosen from the eligible population. Only freemen were eligible to be members or to vote for a member. White, Protestant, landowning adult males were considered freemen. The assembly was permitted to make and pass laws under its own authority, provided those laws were not "contrary or repugnant" to the laws of England. The Charter fixed Rhode Island as a legal entity, with protections both for its inhabitants, as well as for itself as a political reality and physical place.

EARLY ECONOMIC AND CIVIC DEVELOPMENT

Newport was an appealing place to settle due to its geography, landscape and access to natural resources. Its deep, well-protected harbor offered refuge for sailing vessels of all sizes. The waters of the bay and the surrounding ocean were full of fish, and the abundance of trees provided ample timber for the construction of buildings and ships. A freshwater spring only a few hundred yards from the harbor offered a natural advantage for settlement. Newport's development as a major trading center was enhanced by this combination of shelter and resources, as well as its strategic position midway between Boston and New York.

The soil of Aquidneck Island also proved to be fertile. The earliest successes of the inhabitants were built on the ready surplus of hogs, sheep and other livestock, which thrived due to the easy growing conditions for corn, as well as grain. The council seal of Newport would feature a

Henry Bull, one of the original European settlers of Newport, began building his house in 1639 on the east side of the Great Common (later, the site became Spring Street at Bull's Gap). By the time of this photograph, circa 1874, the house had doubled in size. It burned down in 1912. *P391, Collection of the Newport Historical Society.*

sheep as its central motif in recognition of the bountiful nature of the island's agricultural economy. Farming and livestock cultivation allowed the colonists to feed themselves and to produce commodities that could be traded to other towns along the coastline or even farther afield. Red seaweed, which accumulated at certain times of the year and had unique chemical properties that enhanced the growth of crops, was used to fertilize and enrich the island's soil. At first, the colonists followed the style of land-based hierarchy that they had known in England. The initial land grants conveyed status, and as farms and pasturage were developed, families who owned more land became the local gentry.

Agricultural abundance, combined with the tolerant nature of the community, led to rapid growth. Newport went from 100 inhabitants in 1640 to nearly 2,500 by 1680. By 1680, Newport had about four hundred houses, approximately two-thirds of them located within the village itself. The one-room, end-chimney house of the earliest European settlers was replaced by the central-chimney type with at least two rooms on each floor—one noticeably larger than the other. The Wanton-Lyman-Hazard House, built about 1697, is an excellent example of this layout that would later become known as the Rhode Island floor plan. At least five other buildings extant in Newport date in part to before 1700: the Old Stone Mill, the White Horse Tavern, the Great Friends Meeting House, the Elder John Bliss house on Bliss Road and the Bull-Mawdsley house at the corner of Spring and John Streets. After only four decades, there were distinct signs of an emerging prosperous urban society.

The establishment of a stable government in the 1660s only increased the pace of growth. As the town's population grew, the amount of available farmland decreased. With agricultural opportunities limited, residents turned to trade.

In the late 1600s, Newport had extensive trade links with the Caribbean, where the islands were havens for pirates and smugglers. While exact numbers cannot be accurately stated, Newport had its share of mariners who would leave port under the guise of merchants and return with cargoes that had been acquired under dubious circumstances. Some of this was doubtless due to outright piracy, but Newport had also gained a reputation as a haven for smuggling. This disregard for the office of the British customs agent would prove to be a hallmark of the town for at least a century to come. One of the pirates who sailed out of Newport was the infamous Thomas Tew, who used the town as his home port until his death at sea in 1695. The era of piracy proved so troubling to colonial officials

Above: The Wanton-Lyman-Hazard House (circa 1697) as it looks today, under the stewardship of the Newport Historical Society. *Photograph courtesy of the Newport Historical Society.*

Left: An engraving of the infamous pirate Thomas Tew, who sailed out of Newport in the late 1600s. *From* Harper's New Monthly Magazine *89, no. 534 (1894): 812.*

that great efforts were made to curtail it. In 1723, twenty-six pirates were publicly executed by hanging just off Long Wharf in the center of Newport. Their bodies were then taken to Goat Island and buried between the low and high tide marks. This gruesome spectacle undoubtedly did not mark the end of illegal mercantile activities in the colony, but it marked the high point of blatantly lawless commercial behavior.

Newport's economic connections with the Caribbean would also usher in the start of Newport's central role in the trade of enslaved Indigenous people and Africans as merchants sought to increase their wealth and grow Newport's economy.

3

Early Eighteenth Century

Growing Economy and Population

By the mid-eighteenth century, Newport had become the metropolitan center of the colony of Rhode Island. With an ideal climate and a large, accessible harbor, the young village quickly grew, reaching a peak of some nine thousand inhabitants on the cusp of the American Revolution. Craftsmen set up shops to meet the demand for luxury goods for the rapidly developing middle and upper classes of pre-Revolutionary society. The cabinetmakers of Newport would furnish pieces for the salons of the well-heeled residents of the town and would ship fine works of furniture as far afield as Charleston, South Carolina; Annapolis, Maryland; and the Caribbean. In only three years, between 1764 and 1767, 492 chairs, 71 case pieces and 30 tables were shipped from Newport to Annapolis, Maryland, and 133 chairs, 70 case pieces and 30 tables arrived in Charleston, South Carolina, all from Newport. Shipbuilding would also play a prominent role in the town's development, supplying the merchants of Newport with not only local coastal vessels but also deep-draught oceangoing ships from the more than one dozen shipyards located along Aquidneck's southern shores. These ships facilitated Newport's leading role in the transatlantic slave trade, an instrumental component in the rapid commercial expansion during this period.

The Great Meeting House of the Society of Friends (originally constructed in 1699) was the most substantial building in town. New England Quakers

Left: A mahogany and chestnut chest-on-chest made by Newport craftsman John Townsend. *69.3, Collection of the Newport Historical Society.*

Opposite: A map of lots owned by the Quaker proprietors of Easton's Point, 1714–25. *74.17.1a, Collection of the Newport Historical Society.*

built and later enlarged it several times to accommodate their yearly meeting. In the early eighteenth century, Newport Friends had a significant presence with a population of approximately three thousand. In town meeting, the growing Newport community adopted a plan to name its streets in order to aid outsiders and encourage commerce. The town meeting chose John Mumford, a surveyor, to make a map designating streets and roads. In naming the streets in the Point neighborhood, which the Friends owned, the group was influenced by William Penn, the Pennsylvania Quaker who, wishing to avoid "man worship," did not name streets after individuals and renamed the streets of Philadelphia. In the Point neighborhood of Newport, Friends used the names of trees, such as walnut and poplar, in designating the streets running east and west and numbers to indicate those running north and south.

At the turn of the century, land was set aside by the town meeting to support the town school. The new schoolmaster was required to teach three

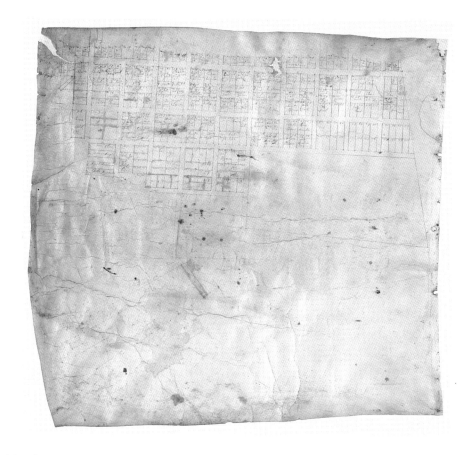

or four orphans for free before benefiting from the land grant endowment. A new school was built at the town's expense, and Newport, with its Latin school and a teacher of the "arts of writing and arithmetic," supported all branches of secondary education that were then in vogue. In his will, Dr. John Clarke stipulated that revenue from his land be used for "schooling children of the poor." In 1676, upon Dr. Clarke's death, the John Clarke Charitable Trust, the earliest and oldest perpetual charitable trust in America, was established. In 1711, the Newport Friends built a school in order to avoid "ye corrupt ways, manners, fashions and Tongue of ye world." There were other private schools in Newport as well. However, some Newport youth attended the well-regarded boarding schools of nearby Boston.

In the early eighteenth century, Newport was a working town. Shipping steadily increased in importance, creating numerous jobs in its related industries. Many men went to sea as mariners in the crews of Newport-based ships. New mills, breweries, distilleries, bakeries, cooperages and tanneries multiplied as trade increased, and the town's volume of shipbuilding compared favorably with that of Boston. Newport shipbuilding was also extremely profitable. Boat builders started with small, inexpensive craft that could be delivered quickly, but these smaller boats were soon supplemented by oceangoing vessels. In 1712, there were more than a dozen shipyards in Newport. Timber was plentiful, and carpenters, joiners, shipwrights and other artisans united in building the tall ships. Ropewalks—which are clearly visible on the maps of the period—and sail lofts employed other skilled artisans. Almost all the six hundred sailing ships owned by the merchants of Newport had been constructed locally.

In addition, Newport vessels became an integral part of the New England whaling fleet. While other prominent merchants on the East Coast are more identified with whaling, Newport entrepreneurs were only too happy to add yet another economic branch to their business empire. At first, whaling ships from Newport simply engaged in the standard practice of hunting the massive seagoing mammals for their blubber, which could be rendered down into valuable oil. However, in the mid-eighteenth century, a Newport merchant named Jacob Rodrigues Rivera perfected a way to transform spermaceti, a waxy substance found in the heads of sperm whales, into a valuable oil. His business produced candles from spermaceti, which burned with less smoke and odor than the more common tallow candles and even more brightly than candles made from beeswax. By the start of the American Revolution, Newport had seventeen such establishments, granting the town a near-monopoly on the production of spermaceti candles made for export.

A reproduction sign for Isaac Stelle's shop specializing in spermaceti. *L93.30.2, Collection of the Newport Historical Society.*

The townsfolk who had employment in Newport were ultimately dependent on farms surrounding the town for their daily bread. As Newport's exports increased, there was more and more demand for the products of millers, bakers, butchers, packers and coopers. At the height of Newport's prominence as a seaport, its waterfront bustled with activity, with over 150 separate wharves and hundreds of shops crowded between Long Wharf and the southern end of the harbor. Merchants brought English goods, as well as molasses, mahogany and raw materials, into Newport and shipped out finished products, such as rum, spermaceti candles and furniture. As Newport's trade throughout the Atlantic Basin grew, the city became an epicenter in the development of modern American capitalism. By the mid-eighteenth century, Newport had become one of the top five ports in colonial America, along with Boston, New York, Philadelphia and Charleston, South Carolina.

Newport and Slavery

In 1696, the Boston ship *Seaflower* landed in Newport Harbor, carrying captives from the coast of Africa; of the forty-seven people forcibly transported on the ship, fourteen were sold in Newport. This introduction of the African slave trade to New England was followed by the first recorded slaving voyage from Newport in 1700, when three vessels departed the town for Africa's western coast. Prior to their entrance into the transatlantic trade, British colonists in New England frequently enslaved Indigenous peoples following clashes with the local Native populations. After both the Pequot War in 1637 and King Philip's War in 1676, Indigenous captives were sold into slavery domestically and exported as labor to the British West Indies.

Participation in the transatlantic slave trade was an integral factor in Newport's swift economic growth in the eighteenth century. Nearly every commercial enterprise during this period was linked to the slave trade. As Newport developed into a center of international trade, new enterprises sprang up to support the explosion of commerce. Nearly every one of these businesses utilized the labor of enslaved men, women and children.

Many of Newport's early settlers retained strong familial, religious and trade connections in the Caribbean. These trade routes grew rapidly in the final years of the seventeenth century, and by the early eighteenth century, Newport had emerged as a key location in the trade networks that crisscrossed the Atlantic. Tropical delights such as citrus fruits made their way into the homes and punch bowls of colonial Newporters. But of all the goods produced in the cradle of the ocean between North and South America, none had a greater role in the development of Atlantic trade (and of Newport itself) than sugar.

The production of sugarcane is inextricably linked to the European colonization of the Caribbean and Americas. The demand for this valuable commodity produced a commercial explosion fueled by desire across

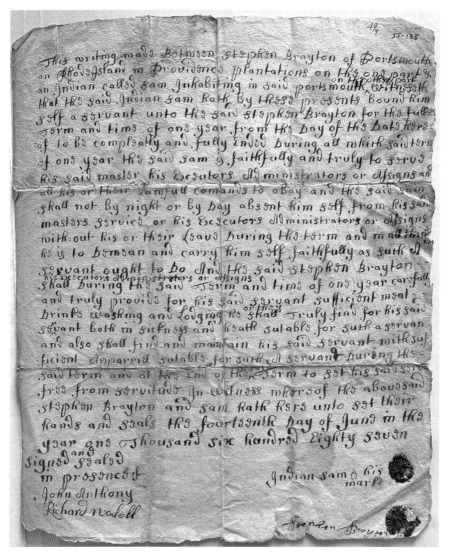

Record of the indenture of Sam, an Indigenous man, to Stephen Brayton, for the span of one year, dated June 14, 1687. *Box 55, folder 9, Collection of the Newport Historical Society.*

the Atlantic world and beyond. Labor-intensive and hazardous to farm and refine, sugar was directly linked to the rapid growth of the trade in enslaved people. As sugar plantations spread across the islands colonized by the French, Dutch, English and Spanish, it became increasingly clear that the style of sugar farming practiced there resulted in a high mortality rate of the enslaved workers due to accidents, disease and maltreatment.

Initially, Indigenous Americans were exploited to work the sugar fields of the Caribbean, but in the early eighteenth century, enslaved Africans became the most common source for this labor.

Merchant traders journeyed to Africa with cargoes of rum and other goods manufactured in colonial Rhode Island, where they traded for enslaved Africans. The ships then sailed to South America, the Caribbean Islands or the American colonies to exchange their human cargo. These enslaved men, women and children would be transported on ships under inhumane conditions, and many died of disease and brutal treatment on the voyage across the Atlantic. Voyages to the West Indies provided sugar plantations with enslaved labor and necessary commodities, including livestock and other provisions. In the Caribbean, the enslaved were typically sold to plantation owners and put to work in sugarcane fields and processing mills, transforming the pressed juice of the cane to molasses. Many of those who were sold in the American colonies by Newport enslavers, ended up working in cotton, tobacco and rice plantations in the South and on farms and in businesses in the North. The traders then returned to Rhode Island ports and sold enslaved people in Newport and molasses to be distilled into rum, and then the process began again.

The rise of the transatlantic trade caused a quick increase in the proliferation and profitability of rum distilling in Newport. According to the diary of Reverend Ezra Stiles, by 1761, the town had sixteen distilleries. Eight years later, this number had grown to twenty-two. Many Newport residents had an interest in lucrative businesses like rum distilling, which was directly tied to the enslavement of Africans. Even Reverend Nathaniel Coggeshall of the Second Congregational Church on Clarke Street was a part-owner of one of these distilleries. At this time, there was one distillery for every 409 residents of the town. At the peak of the town's maritime ascendency, after the end of the Seven Years' War, some fourteen thousand hogsheads of molasses were brought into the port. These distilleries were just a few examples of the many business concerns that profited from the wealth that the trade in enslaved persons brought to the community.

Along with molasses and other products, enslaved men, women and children were brought to Newport and sold to its residents. By 1755, people of African descent, both enslaved and free, accounted for 18 percent of Newport's total residents. The 1774 census shows that roughly one-third of middle-class families in Newport enslaved at least one person; some families enslaved five or more people. Enslaved people usually lived in the households of their enslavers. Many of them worked for wages, which were

Families	Whites				Newport Indians				Blacks				Tot.
	Males		Females		Males		Females		Males		Females		
	above 16	under 16	above 16	under 16	above 16	under 16	above 16	under 16	above 16	under 16	above 16	under 16	
Aaron Lopez	9	2	7	7			1		4		1		31
John Tweedy	2								2		1		5
William Ladd	1	4	2	1									8
Christopher Champlin	1	1	4	2					1		1		10
John Bours	2	1	2	1					1				8
John Megœ	4	1	1	1					3		1		11
Joshua Amy	1			1					1	1	1		5
Ann Dwarehouse	1		2										4
John Proud	2		2										4
Robert Bagnall	1		3	1									5
Charles Reake	2		1										3
Sarah Sparkes			1										1
John Bell	1	2	2	5					1		2		13
George Gibbs	2		3	4					3		2	1	15
Jabez Champlin	1		2	1					1	1	1		7
Lemuel Crandall	1	2	3										6
Thomas Arnold	1	0	2	1							1		5
Thomas Cranston	1	1							2	1	1	2	9
Joseph Wanton	3		1	1					3	1	2		11
Standfast Wyatt	2	2	4	2			1				1		12
Elnathan Hammond	1		1						1		1		4

This page, top: A page from the *1774 Colony of Rhode Island Census*, showing tallies of enslaved Black and Indigenous people in Newport households. *The Rhode Island State Archives.*

This page, bottom: This overmantel painting (circa 1740) features South County plantation owner John Potter, his family and an unidentified enslaved boy. Slavery and the slave trade undergirded the entire colonial economy in Newport and the state of Rhode Island. The inclusion of this child in the portrait of the Potter family taking tea was likely meant to demonstrate their upper-class status. *53.3, Collection of the Newport Historical Society.*

Opposite: Abraham Casey's account with Newport merchant Aaron Lopez. On the left side of the account, Lopez lists the cocoa beans he provided. The amount of chocolate ground by Casey, an enslaved man, is noted on the right. *Collection of the Newport Historical Society, vol. 715, section 37.*

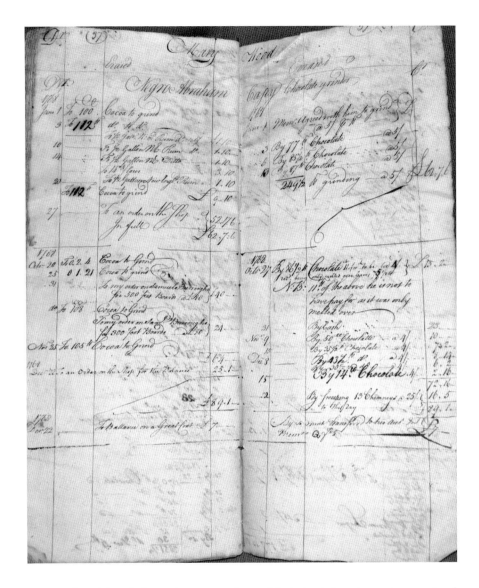

appropriated by their enslavers, and provided the labor-intensive work of farm labor and running colonial homes.

As well as participating in the trade in enslaved individuals, Newport merchants uniformly used the labor of enslaved people in both skilled and unskilled jobs in the town's businesses. Many individuals in Newport's enslaved community became highly skilled craftspeople. Duchess Quamino, enslaved in the Channing household, was renowned for her cooking and baking skills. Prince Updike was hired out to Aaron Lopez by the Updike

The northern section of Newport's Common Burying Ground is referred to as God's Little Acre. It is the largest intact colonial-era African burial ground in the United States and contains many graves from the postcolonial period. *Photograph courtesy of Kaela Bleho.*

family for his expertise in chocolate grinding. Zingo Stevens carved headstones that still stand in God's Little Acre, the area of the Common Burying Ground that contains the marked graves of nearly five hundred free and enslaved people of African descent. Established in 1665 by the Town of Newport, the Common Burying Ground is located on the outskirts of the colonial boundaries of the town; God's Little Acre is located at the northern boundary. These graves mark a few of the many people of African descent, enslaved and free, who lived and worked in Newport during the era of slavery. By the late eighteenth century, Newport had a significant free Black population; the 1790 census of Rhode Island recorded 417 free Black residents in the town of Newport, or just over 6 percent of the total population. See chapter 6 for more information on the Black community in Newport during this period.

Elsewhere in Rhode Island, by the mid-eighteenth century, between one-fourth and one-third of the enslaved population of the colony worked on the agricultural plantations in southern Rhode Island. The large farms there produced foodstuffs and livestock that were directly exported to support the sugar plantations of the West Indies.

Eighteenth-Century Town Life

Like so many other features of seventeenth- and eighteenth-century Newport, the town's development as a trading port followed religious pathways. In the 1650s, both Quakers and Jews came to Newport in search of religious toleration. Most of the Jews were Sephardic. They had been expelled from Spain or Portugal in 1492 when Christians forced Muslims out as well. These Jewish immigrants came to Newport by way of Barbados, Jamaica, Surinam, Curaçao and Amsterdam; the Quakers came from Barbados, New York and England. Jewish and Quaker merchants continued to communicate with their former communities for religious and commercial reasons. Both groups dominated the town's maritime trade until the 1760s; they included men like Aaron Lopez and Abraham Redwood, two of Newport's wealthiest residents.

By the mid-eighteenth century, the religious diversity that grew out of Newport's practice of toleration was still unique in comparison with the surrounding colonies. Religion and family combined to become the most powerful influences on life in Newport, shaping business relationships, marriage prospects and political views. By 1750, there were three different Baptist congregations, along with Congregationalists, Quakers, Jews, Anglicans and Moravians, all thriving in Newport. A few French Huguenots also immigrated to Newport and settled in the town. By the mid-eighteenth century, the population had momentarily stabilized at 6,508 in 1748 and 6,733 in 1755. The governor of Rhode Island reported back to England, "We have lately a few or no newcomers either of English, Scotch, Irish, or foreigners." Shortly afterward, however, the population of Newport began to rise again, reaching 9,209 in 1774.

In this period, taverns, victual houses and grog shops multiplied in Newport to meet the demands of the growing town. Approximately twenty taverns were licensed annually. The White Horse Tavern, in particular, was a popular gathering place. The Quakers, whose meetinghouse was located across the street, would drop in after their meeting; the Town Council convened there in 1712; and the Rhode Island General Assembly held meetings there in 1713. Taverns in colonial America were not only places to eat and drink; they also housed travelers, who, in turn, brought news from the wider world. Other excellent public houses served sumptuous meals; Palmer, Mallet and Melville were notable hosts. Whiting's King's Arms was a place where prominent merchants and shipbuilders could transact business. The proprietors of some taverns were women. Mary Cowley ran the Crown

The White Horse Tavern, at the corner of Farewell and Marlborough Streets, 1874. *P388, Collection of the Newport Historical Society.*

Coffee House on Church Street, and Sarah Bright provided a billiard table, a nine-pin alley and a large garden at her establishment.

Newport's trade networks, prosperity, culture, climate and accessibility drew summer visitors from the West Indies, Charleston and Philadelphia. Travelers also arrived from England, Scotland, Ireland and continental Europe. Plantation owners from South Carolina discovered Newport to be a refreshing haven from the heat and disease prevalent in summer weather in the South. Prominent South Carolinians who came in this period included the Izards, Manigaults and Middletons; those from Philadelphia included the Whartons, Biddles, Nichols, Rawles and Mifflins. The enterprising Samuel Hall at the *Newport Mercury* and his successor, Solomon Southwick, were the first journalists in America to introduce reportage on summer visitors in a prototype society column. In addition to the commercial news of ship arrivals and departures, in the summer, the *Mercury* included a list of persons arriving or leaving for the season, then designated as the months of July and August.

This panel is believed to be from the first fire pumper in Newport, imported from the English company Newsham & Ragg in 1736. Judging from the bunting showing thirteen stripes, the panel was painted sometime after 1776. *91.7.36, Collection of the Newport Historical Society.*

Another sign of the town's prosperity was the establishment of a fire company. The town of Newport passed ordinances similar to those in other towns in New England that required households to own a leather fire bucket stenciled with the family's name. A threatening blaze in 1705 that broke out in a smithy was confined to one nearby house. The greatest scare came in February 1730, when a fire on Malbone's Wharf destroyed a cooper's shop and six warehouses. An eyewitness related that there was no loss of life, and a general fire was prevented "through God's wonderful mercy."

Soon after, Newport's wealthiest citizen, Godfrey Malbone, donated a state-of-the-art fire engine, made in London, for the general use of the town. Named *Torrent No. 1*, it was a suction-pump engine. Despite this precaution, Malbone's own dwelling at his country estate at the foot of present-day Miantonomi Hill burned to the ground in 1766. Citizens formed associations with names such as "Hand-in-Hand," "United," "Rough and Ready," "Hercules," "Hope," "Protection" and "Deluge" that functioned as volunteer fire companies to protect the town against devastating conflagrations. Fortunately for its citizens, Newport managed to avoid the sort of disastrous fires that leveled other towns of its size and wealth in this period.

4

The Cultural Life of Eighteenth-Century Newport

Intellectual Pursuits

The seeds of culture often thrive in wealth, and this was true in eighteenth-century Newport, where riches accrued to many prominent merchants either directly or indirectly from profits in the business of slavery. Abraham Redwood, principal benefactor of the Redwood Library, owned a sugar plantation in the West Indies that was entirely dependent on the labor of enslaved people. Redwood also used enslaved workers in his home and businesses in Newport. Ezra Stiles, the esteemed minister of the Second Congregational Church, invested in voyages to Africa and purchased enslaved people for his household. A host of prominent Newport merchants used their wealth to support the artistic, intellectual and cultural life of the town, and residents, like George Berkeley and Ezra Stiles, provided a level of intellectual discourse that enriched the entire community.

George Berkeley, the Anglo-Irish philosopher and clergyman who was Dean of Derry in Ireland, formed a plan to start a college in Bermuda in order to train Anglican ministers in America and to educate Indigenous Americans. While waiting in vain for Parliament to fund the project, Berkeley came to Newport, where he joined the congregation of Trinity Church. In 1729, he purchased land and built a home, which he called Whitehall, in what is now Middletown. To assist him with work at Whitehall, Berkeley purchased three enslaved people, whom he baptized in Trinity Church,

George Berkeley, a noted philosopher and Bishop of Cloyne, Ireland. *2004.13.110, Collection of the Newport Historical Society.*

naming them Philip, Anthony and Agnes Berkeley. Hanging Rock, a striking geographical feature not far from the house, is said to be the site where Berkeley wrote one of his better-known works, *The Alciphron.*

Berkeley also brought with him a coterie of intellectuals and artists who included John Smibert, the painter. These recent arrivals found an active group of successful merchants in Newport, including Abraham Redwood, Henry Collins and others who helped mold the town into a center of culture.

Berkeley returned home in 1731 and was later consecrated Bishop of Cloyne. He donated Whitehall to Yale University when he departed. During his short stay in America, he was active in forming a literary and philosophical society. Some of this group became founders and charter members of the Redwood Library and Athenaeum between 1746 and 1747. Abraham Redwood, gave £500 sterling to be used to purchase "suitable" books for a "Library...having nothing in view but the Good of Mankind." Redwood persuaded his fellow incorporators to build the library on land that was donated by another wealthy merchant, Henry Collins. The library's original book collection was purchased in London but was dispersed during the Revolution. It was reassembled after the war and is now largely intact.

Above: The Redwood Library and Athenaeum, designed by Peter Harrison, was constructed between 1748 and 1749. This color lithograph dates between 1858 and 1875. *2008.6.2, Collection of the Newport Historical Society.*

Left: The Franklin printing press. Moved to Boston from London by James Franklin in 1717, the press was brought to Newport in 1726. *L 93.54.1, on loan to the Newport Historical Society from the Massachusetts Charitable Mechanic Association.*

The Redwood opened in 1750 and remains the oldest subscription library in America to survive in its original building.

The Newport community, with an excellent library to foster literary and philosophical discourse, also supported an enlightened press. James Franklin, the elder brother of Benjamin Franklin, was the first printer in Newport. He had previously published the *New England Courant*, a Boston newspaper noted for supporting unpopular causes. Soon after the *Courant* was forced to close, James moved his press to Newport, and in 1732, he established the Franklin Press and started the *Rhode Island Gazette*, the first newspaper printed in Rhode Island. After James Franklin's death in 1735, his widow, Ann, continued operating the Franklin Press, bringing up her daughters and son as printers. In 1758, Ann Franklin and her son James Jr. began to publish the *Newport Mercury*. James Franklin Jr. died in 1761, and Ann took on Samuel Hall as a business partner. After Ann Franklin's death in 1763, Hall took control of the press and the *Newport Mercury*. In 1768, Hall sold the press and paper to Solomon Southwick, who later published the journal under the motto "Undaunted by TYRANTS we'll DIE or be FREE." A varied collection of literary works and broadsides carried the imprint of these early Newport printers.

No account of Newport's cultural life during the eighteenth century would be complete without including Ezra Stiles, the minister who was called to the Second Congregational Church in 1756. Stiles was also elected Librarian of the Redwood Library. After fleeing Newport on the eve of the British occupation during the Revolution, Stiles went on to become one of Yale University's most distinguished early presidents. The diaries that he kept while in Newport reveal a truly brilliant, cosmopolitan intellect and record many fascinating details about life in Newport in the mid- to late eighteenth century.

ART AND ARCHITECTURE

Artist John Smibert, who came to Newport with Berkeley in 1729, responded to an increasing demand for portraits for leading merchants, lawyers and civic leaders. These prosperous town residents wished to display their social status by commissioning portraits of themselves and their families. Robert Feke, born in Oyster Bay, Long Island, also received a number of portrait commissions in Newport. Both of these early Newport artists had a strong influence on later American portrait painters. Other artists who worked in Newport included Joseph Blackburn, followed by post-Revolutionary or Federal period painters, such as Gilbert Stuart, Washington Allston, Michele Felice Cornè, Samuel King and Charles Bird King. Newport portrait miniaturist Edward Greene Malbone's work was also greatly prized.

Newport experienced a remarkable flowering in architecture as well during this period. By the mid-eighteenth century, buildings were erected that both signaled and served the growing wealth and prominence of the community. A grand civic building known as the Colony House, built in 1740, dominated the Parade, or town square. The Rhode Island General Assembly, which rotated between Newport, Providence, Kingston, East Greenwich and Bristol, met here until the early twentieth century, when

The Colony House (circa 1885), designed by Richard Munday, was built between 1739 and 1744. It was the principal seat of the Rhode Island government before the Revolution. After 1780, the Colony House served as one of five Rhode Island statehouses until 1902, when the new statehouse opened in Providence. *P8620, Collection of the Newport Historical Society.*

the current Rhode Island statehouse in Providence was completed. At the opposite end, at the head of Long Wharf, a public market (now known as the Brick Market) was constructed in a classical design. Both structures are still standing as of this writing.

With the government building at the head of the Parade and a building for public commerce at the foot, the only missing structure, according to a typical New England plan, was a central church. This deliberate omission of a house of worship on the "common" land at the heart of the town emphasized the town's commitment to religious diversity. Many of Newport's eighteenth-century buildings survive to this day, displaying classic Georgian and Neoclassical architectural features. The leading merchants of the town lived in homes planned using the most advanced architectural designs of the age. A view of the town painted in the 1740s revealed a bustling community, with multiple churches and large homes visible from the harbor. Another contemporary map of the town depicted broad streets laid out in a regular pattern, all of which led down to the public and private wharves that generated much of Newport's wealth.

In the town's earliest days, buildings were designed by either their owners or anonymous "housewrights." But by the mid-eighteenth century, master

Newport, R.I. in 1730. A nineteenth-century color lithograph of an eighteenth-century overmantel painting (artist unknown). Although titled *Newport in 1730*, the image more closely illustrates Newport circa 1740, as it depicts the Colony House (completed by 1744). *01.953, Collection of the Newport Historical Society.*

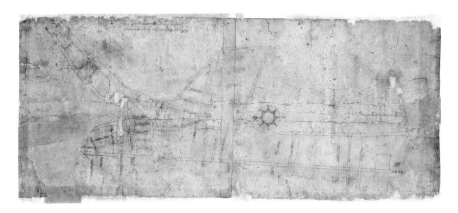

Above: A handwritten map of the town of Newport drawn by John Mumford, circa 1712. The map features several Newport streets and wharves, including Thames, Broad (Broadway), Bull, Clarke and Spring Streets. *2006.8, Collection of the Newport Historical Society.*

Left: Trinity Church on Spring Street was designed by Richard Munday and erected in 1725–26. The steeple was part of the initial design but was not added until 1741, after Munday had died. Rebuilt in 1768, it is one of the only intact eighteenth-century wooden church steeples of its kind in the country. *P674, Collection of the Newport Historical Society.*

Touro Synagogue, erected between 1759 and 1763, is one of Newport's three important buildings designed by Peter Harrison in the Palladian style. *P2763, Collection of the Newport Historical Society.*

builders and architects began to create homes and public buildings following the latest styles popular in England and Europe. Richard Munday's Trinity Church (1725–26), Seventh Day Baptist Meeting House (1730) and the Colony House (1739–44) are lasting monuments to his taste and skill. Munday was a master builder influenced by Sir Christopher Wren, the English royal architect who gained an international reputation for his work rebuilding London after the Great Fire in 1666.

Peter Harrison, a merchant by trade who followed Munday as the chosen designer of important public buildings in Newport, worked in a more austere classical style. Often described as America's first architect, Harrison was a gentleman architect—essentially a self-educated sea captain capable of using architectural books to plan buildings. Harrison designed the Redwood Library (1748–50), Touro Synagogue (1759–63) and the Brick Market (1762–72) in Newport, as well as Christ Church in Cambridge, Massachusetts, and King's Chapel in Boston. He amassed an impressive library of books on architecture. Many of these works contained drawings that illustrated the latest English fascination with Roman and Greek antiquity where he found inspiration. Harrison was the first true interpreter of the work of Italian Renaissance architect Andrea Palladio in America; the purified classical design of Harrison's buildings seemed avant-garde at the time.

MUSIC AND AMUSEMENTS

Bishop George Berkeley's gift of an organ to Trinity Church in 1733 enriched Newport's musical offerings. The church's first organist was Charles Theodore Pachelbel, son of the famed German baroque composer Johann Pachelbel. The *Newport Mercury* carried advertisements in 1774 noting that Charles Pachelbel's successor as Trinity's organist, William Selby, "just arrived from London…would instruct young Gentlemen and Ladies to play upon the violin, flute, harpsichord, guitar, and other instruments." Concerts by Boston musicians were not infrequent, and private concerts could be arranged.

Dancing was a favorite amusement in colonial Newport. As early as 1745, thirteen local bachelors formed an assembly and issued invitations to thirty-two "qualified young ladies." Dancing schools increased, and French dancing masters advertised. Dinners were often followed by dancing, along with cards, backgammon and billiards. "Turtle Frolics" were very popular as summer entertainment. Cuffee, a man enslaved by Jahleel Brenton, was in

The organ purchased for Trinity Church by Bishop Berkeley and Mr. Honyman in 1733.
91.41.1, Collection of the Newport Historical Society.

great demand as a cook for these affairs, where he "prepared the principal delicacy, a turtle soup." These frolics were usually held on Goat Island near Fort George and went on from early afternoon until they closed with a hot toddy around midnight.

COLONIAL MEDICINE

Medical men played an important role in the civic life of colonial Newport. Dr. Benjamin Waterhouse, one of the founders of Harvard Medical School and a professor there, was a Newporter who made medical history in the fight against smallpox, which was a lethal infectious disease at the time. Born in Newport in 1754, he was educated in Newport's Trinity Church School and received his first medical training from Dr. John Halliburton, also of Newport. Waterhouse was the first physician to vaccinate for smallpox in the colonies. Thomas Moffat and William Hunter, both from Scotland, were two other noted medical practitioners in Newport during this period. To supplement his income during his early years in practice, Moffat bought a snuff mill in North Kingstown that was operated by the father of artist Gilbert Stuart. The Stuart family moved to Newport, where Gilbert also studied at the Trinity Church School. Moffat's brother, John, who sold artists' supplies, encouraged the young Stuart in his painting.

****

An ACT permitting Inoculation for the Small-Pox in this Colony.

Act permitting Inoculation.

WHEREAS the Small-Pox hath made the moſt dreadful Ravages in the Army lately before *Quebec*, which was a principal Cauſe of raiſing the Blockade of that City, and there is great Danger that the Inhabitants of the United Colonies may, by the Prevalence of that dreadful Diſtemper, be rendered incapable of Defence at a Time when their Safety may depend upon their moſt vigorous Exertions : And whereas that Diſtemper taken by Inoculation is ſo eaſy and light, and the Method of Treatment ſo beneficial, that any Number of Perſons inoculated are more likely to live, than the ſame Number of Perſons not inoculated; and as by introducing the Practice of Inoculation with Prudence and Caution, the greater Part of the male Inhabitants of the Colonies may ſoon get over that terrible Diſeaſe, and the fatal Conſequences to be apprehended from our Armies being infected therewith be averted :

In June 1776, the Rhode Island General Assembly voted to permit inoculation for smallpox in the state. John G. Wanton of Newport was one of ten assembly members who protested the bill's passage; they maintained that the community had not been fully informed, that inoculation had been abandoned in other places and that a provision had not been made for the poor, who made up the largest segment of the community. *F76 R4 1776–77 V.13, Collection of the Newport Historical Society.*

ARTISANS AND CRAFTSMEN

By the mid-eighteenth century, a large class of artisans and craftsmen in Newport were producing goods for consumption both locally and abroad. Their work, which often depended on the labor of enslaved people, contributed significantly to the prosperity of Newport. Historians estimate that, during the 1760s, ninety-nine cabinetmakers, seventeen chair-makers and two upholsterers plied their trades in Newport. Other woodworkers included four carvers, one turner and sixteen joiners. The silversmiths Arnold Collins, Samuel Vernon, Benjamin Brenton, John Coddington and Daniel Russell worked early in the eighteenth century, while John Tanner, Jonathan Otis, Walter Cornell, Nicholas Geoffroy and William Nichols worked in the late eighteenth century and into the nineteenth century. The business of the great clockmaking family of William and Thomas Claggett, along with James Wady, flourished during most of the eighteenth century.

The best-known Newport craftsmen were members of the Townsend and Goddard families, whose cabinets and chairs, clock cases and other pieces of furniture were recognized as supreme examples of craftsmanship. Job Townsend (1699–1765) and his brother Christopher started the family cabinetmaking business. (*Cabinetmaker* was a term for an artisan who made furniture.) Job's daughter Hannah married John Goddard (1732–1783) and three of their fifteen children became excellent cabinetmakers. In all, there were eight Townsends and six Goddards who were master craftsmen. Much of the furniture made in Newport during this period was crafted for installation on ships that were built here, shipment into the inland interior or export via the intercolonial coastal trade. The rest graced Newport houses, and some local families have owned either Townsend or Goddard pieces for more than two centuries.

Wall clock by William Claggett, dating to around 1743; it was installed in the Seventh Day Baptist Meeting House. Claggett was one of the first Newport clockmakers to machine his own clockworks. *1884.4, Collection of the Newport Historical Society.*

The marriage of Quaum, enslaved by silversmith Jonathan Otis, and Lilly, enslaved by William Ellery. *Second Congregational Church Records* [Newport], *January 10, 1774, vol. 838, 72, Collection of the Newport Historical Society.*

Most of the artisans who lived in Newport supplied a wide range of products to Newport residents—not only to the wealthy merchant class. Some craftsmen became merchants and sea captains. With its culture, refinement and wealth, Newport had become a cosmopolitan town where many inhabitants lived in comfort and affluence. More frequent enforcement of the British Navigation Acts, however, threatened Newport's economic prosperity, and the eve of the Revolution found a number of Newport residents opposed to British regulations.

5

REVOLUTIONARY WAR ERA

PRELUDE TO REVOLUTION

Tensions between Rhode Islanders and Great Britain existed from almost the founding of the colony, particularly regarding trade. During the French and Indian War (1754–63), Rhode Island merchants traded with Great Britain's enemy, France. This and other violations of British regulations led to the establishment of laws that imposed new taxes on the American colonies. The 1764 Sugar Act created a high duty on imported sugar and molasses; prohibited the importation of all foreign rum; and taxed wine, coffee and textiles. The Sugar Act directly interfered with Rhode Island's economy, which was heavily dependent on the importation of molasses and the export of rum. However, Rhode Island merchants found ways to evade the tax, so British ships were sent to patrol Narragansett Bay and adjacent harbors, wreaking havoc on local shipping.

Violence broke out in 1764, when the customs schooner HMS *St. John* confiscated illicit cargo from a Newport merchant ship. Angry townsfolk seized control of Fort George on Goat Island and opened fire on the schooner. Though the shots missed, this incident marked the first in a series of violent responses to British interference with colonial shipping. Shortly afterward, a British officer who was landing from a boat at Malbone's Wharf on the trail of a deserter was seized by a mob, and the boat's crew was stoned. The protestors took a sloop into the harbor intending to board *St. John* but withdrew when the twenty-gun HMS *Squirrel* appeared. During the following summer, HMS *Maidstone*, on anti-smuggling duty in the harbor, landed in town to capture a deserter. A British press gang took the entire crew of one brig, but a mob of citizens seized the press gang's longboat, dragged it to the Parade and burned it. The following spring, the British Parliament enacted the Stamp Act. The tax required colonists to pay for stamps to be placed on paper products, including newspapers, pamphlets, legal documents and even playing cards, which enraged citizens even more.

Not all residents of Newport opposed the rule of British law, however. During the 1760s, a small but vocal cadre of Loyalist citizens publicly supported policies of the British Crown. Known as the "Newport Junto," they included prominent members of local society. One of their number, a lawyer named Martin Howard, wrote a pamphlet titled "A Letter from a Gentleman at Halifax," which laid out arguments in support of Parliament's right to levy taxes on the American colonies. These sentiments, expressed in 1765 as the furor against the Stamp Act was building, made Howard few friends in Newport. Appointed as one of the stamp collectors for Newport, Howard was driven out of town in 1765 by an angry mob, which hanged him in effigy, ransacked his home and destroyed his personal possessions. Another staunch Newport Tory, Dr. John Moffat, served as one of the commissioners of the Stamp Act. During the Stamp Act riots of 1765, a mob sacked Moffat's Newport house and forced him to flee. He took refuge in the house of Quaker Thomas Robinson on Washington Street. Once the riots were over, Moffat made his way to New London, Connecticut. From there, Moffat fled to London and never returned to Newport.

The Stamp Act was defeated by popular outcry from across the thirteen colonies, but Parliament would not end its efforts to regain some of the

Last Tuesday Morning a Gallows was erected in Queen-Street, just below the Court-House, whereon the Effigies of three Gentlemen were exhibited, one of whom was a Distributor of Stamps, which was placed in the Center. The other two were suspected of countenancing and abetting the Stamp Act.—— Various Labels were affixed to their Breasts, Arms, &c, denoting the Cause of these indignant Representations, and the Persons who were the Subjects of Derision.—— They hung from Eleven o'Clock till about Four, when some Combustibles being placed under the Gallows, a Fire was made, and the Effigies consumed, amidst the Acclamations of the People.——The whole was conducted with Moderation, and no Violence offered to the Persons or Property of any Man.

An excerpt from the *Newport Mercury*, September 2, 1765, reporting on protests against Newport leaders who condoned the Stamp Act. *Photograph courtesy of the Newport Historical Society.*

The Burning of the Gaspee, oil on canvas painting by Charles DeWolf Brownell, 1892. *RHi X5 10, Rhode Island Historical Society.*

money it spent in Britain's American wars. Newport's own band of the Sons of Liberty—which organized and led many of the protests against the Stamp Act—rejoiced in the repeal of the law. In celebration, they dedicated a Liberty Tree on a small plot of land just off Farewell Street. This location served as their meeting place until the British army and navy occupied the town a little over a decade later.

In Newport, popular resistance to British customs law remained strong, and smuggling continued at a feverish pace. The British admiralty dispatched more vessels to try to rein in illegal trade. In 1769, the armed sloop *Liberty*, which patrolled Narragansett Bay, was seized by anti-British protesters and scuttled near Long Wharf, the commercial center of Newport Harbor. Although an official protest was made to the Admiralty in London, the authorities decided to quietly let the event pass by in the hopes that their reluctance to prosecute the offenders would ease tensions in Rhode Island. Perhaps the most noted pre–Revolutionary War resistance to British authority on Narragansett Bay occurred in 1772, when HMS *Gaspee*, a ship patrolling the bay, ran aground off Warwick. Patriots from Providence boarded the stranded vessel and shot and injured its commander, Lieutenant William Dudingston. The Americans set the *Gaspee* on fire and arrested Dudingston and his sailors.

In 1775, three years after the *Gaspee* incident, Captain James Wallace, in command of HMS *Rose*, arrived off Newport; his mission was to curb smuggling. The *Rose* threatened Newport, and its captain demanded livestock and other supplies be taken by force if necessary. Instead of bombarding Newport, however, Wallace raided the coastal communities of Bristol, Jamestown, Block Island, Stonington and New London. The Rhode Island General Assembly ordered the removal of the cannon and gunpowder from Fort George on Goat Island in Newport Harbor. It also established Rhode Island's own navy, consisting of the sloop *Katy*, commanded by Abraham Whipple. *Katy* completed the removal of the guns. Soon afterward, the vessel was renamed *Providence* and transferred to the Continental Navy. The Navy was established on October 13, 1775, after the General Assembly took the initiative and instructed its delegates in Congress to promote the creation of a national navy. Rhode Islander Esek Hopkins was made its commander-in-chief, and several Newport men took important posts in the naval hierarchy. Newport lawyer and delegate to Congress William Ellery was appointed to the Marine Committee of Congress, and William Vernon, also from Newport, became the commissioner of the Navy Board, Eastern District. John Hazard took command of the *Providence* when Abraham Whipple was given a larger ship in the new fleet. In May 1776, Hazard was relieved of duty for poor performance, and John Paul Jones assumed command of the *Providence*.

WAR AND OCCUPATION

When British forces engaged local militiamen in Lexington and Concord in April 1775, Newport residents quickly joined in the wider cause for American independence. Its citizens celebrated the news of the British withdrawal from Boston in March 1776. Despite rejoicing from the Patriots in town, the Royal Navy was still an active presence in Narragansett Bay, as its officers continued to seize suspect ships and their cargoes. There were also a significant number of "Tories," or British sympathizers, still remaining in Newport.

On May 4, 1776, Rhode Island became the first of the thirteen colonies to formally renounce its oath of loyalty to King George III. When William Ellery signed the Declaration of Independence, which was passed by the Continental Congress in Philadelphia in July 1776, the British government

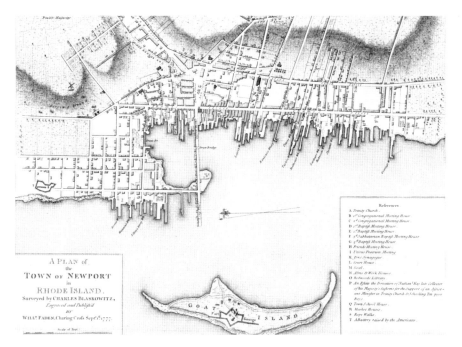

A Plan of the Town of Newport in Rhode Island Surveyed by Charles Blaskowitz. The map was commissioned by the British occupiers of Newport and was engraved and published by William Faden on September 4, 1777. *01.952, Collection of the Newport Historical Society.*

set its sights on Newport. Requiring a new port for its navy after its eviction from Boston, Parliament now considered Newport a prime naval base. In December 1776, a British ship sailed into the waters of Narragansett Bay, carrying soldiers under the command of General Henry Clinton. With a British fleet in the harbor and an army quartered in the city, many Newport residents and their families, both Patriot and Tory, fled to Massachusetts, northern Rhode Island and other locales where they felt safer. The local population dropped from about 11,000 in 1775 to 5,300 in 1776.

After the French Treaty of Alliance was ratified in 1778, and Holland and Spain joined France as allies, England found itself fighting a major world war. Two months later, the Comte d'Estaing arrived off Newport with a large French fleet to assist General John Sullivan and the Continental army in attacking British-held Newport. The British prepared for a long siege by concentrating their forces in earthworks around Newport. The French ships forced their way into the bay, exchanging gunfire with the guns placed near Castle Hill. French soldiers landed on Conanicut Island (Jamestown) and then moved to land at Portsmouth. As the French and Americans moved

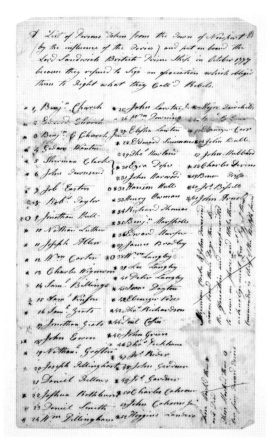

Left: "A List of Persons Taken from the Town of Newport by the Influence of the Tories and Put on Board the Lord Sandwich British Prison Ship in October 1777." During the British occupation of Newport, men suspected of being anti-British (or pro-American) were arrested and held on a prison ship in Newport Harbor. *Box 123, folder 21, Collection of the Newport Historical Society.*

Below: The First Rhode Island Regiment was an integrated unit. Approximately three-quarters of the men in the First Rhode Island Regiment were of African descent, both enslaved and free; the other soldiers were white and Indigenous. Those who were enslaved were promised their freedom after the conclusion of the war. This illustration by Jean Baptiste Antoine de Verger is dated to 1781. *2021669876, Library of Congress.*

into position to begin their operation against Newport, Admiral Lord Howe and British naval forces learned of the French presence and gathered in Rhode Island Sound. Fearing that he would become trapped in the bay, d'Estaing broke off the landing in Portsmouth. With his squadron, he fought his way out past Castle Hill, intending to engage Howe in a major fleet battle. Before they could get into position, both fleets were hit by an August hurricane, and they dispersed.

After making temporary repairs at sea off the Delaware coast, d'Estaing returned to Newport to confer with Sullivan, but at that point, it was clear that the French ships were too badly damaged to attempt to attack the entrenched British army at Newport. They instead moved on to Boston to spend two months undergoing further repairs.

Deprived of French assistance, an American force under General Sullivan, which was waiting on the outskirts of Newport, was forced to retreat. The Battle of Rhode Island, the only major land engagement in Rhode Island, was fought on August 29, 1778, at the northern end of Aquidneck Island. The Patriot army included the First Rhode Island Regiment of the Continental line under Colonel Christopher Greene. This unit, which fought in every engagement of the Revolution except two, was desperately under strength at the time of the battle. Unlike virtually all the other units, this one was composed largely of men of African descent and Native Americans, both free and enslaved. Some had enlisted voluntarily, while others had been offered for service by their enslavers, who were then financially compensated for their loss of labor. The First Rhode Island Regiment's bravery during the Battle of Rhode Island is commemorated by a memorial located in Portsmouth on Route 114.

This cannonball, found on the Henry Hedley Farm in Portsmouth, is thought to have been fired during the Battle of Rhode Island on August 29, 1778. The battle was the only one fought in Rhode Island during the war. *FIC.2016.028, Collection of the Newport Historical Society.*

The American forces fought valiantly at what is now called "Bloody Brook" in Portsmouth but could not dislodge the British. They retreated across the Sakonnet River to the mainland. They remained there until October 1779, when British forces withdrew from Newport in an attempt to consolidate their forces in and around New York City as part of their new "southern strategy."

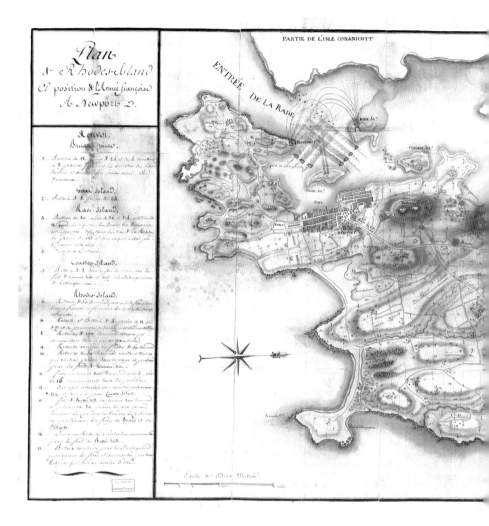

When the British army and navy left, Newport's glory days as a seaport lay in the ruins of the shattered town. The British occupiers had destroyed or damaged hundreds of homes and businesses in Newport. Its population was reduced to half its prewar level. The harbor, once a welcome shelter for merchant vessels, was littered with ships that were sunk deliberately by the British to block the seaward approaches. Newport's churches had been used as barracks or hospitals. Only Trinity Church, an Anglican house of worship that was used as the garrison church by the British army, was spared much damage.

The Colony House, which had been a barracks and hospital under the British, was in such bad repair that it was boarded up. After the evacuation

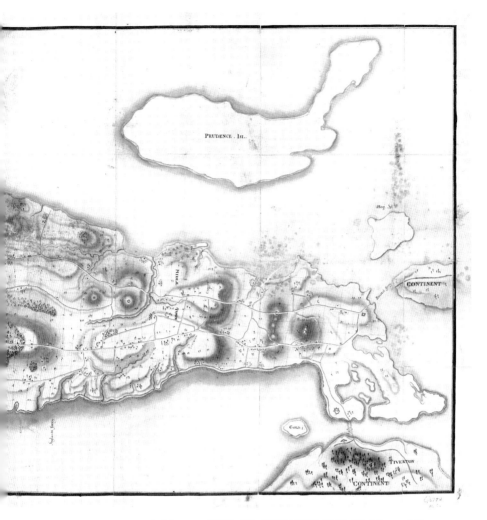

A French encampment in Newport (1780–81). *G3774.N4S3 1780. P5, Library of Congress.*

of the British, the town meeting had to convene in Touro Synagogue. In October 1779, the departing British forces took important town documents with them. When the ship carrying these essential town records ran aground and foundered en route to New York, the records were submerged. However, the documents were quickly recovered and stored in wet boxes for three years before they were returned to Newport.

On July 10, 1780, a new fleet arrived in the waters of Narragansett Bay. Several regiments of the French army commanded by the Comte de Rochambeau were on board the ships that sailed into Newport Harbor after much negotiation between American agents and the Court of Versailles. The ships carried thousands of soldiers to reinforce the Continental army and a multitude of military supplies. The vessels ranged from huge line-of-battle warships to lumbering transports. The troops and their aristocratic officers had spent seventy-one days at sea.

At first, inhabitants of Newport offered the Comte de Rochambeau and his men an unenthusiastic welcome. Newport had suffered greatly under the British occupation, and its residents feared that the French would further disrupt the fragile recovery of the town. The Frenchmen, formerly America's enemies who were also Catholics, were eyed with suspicion. Eventually, official representatives from Congress and the Continental army arrived and made proper introductions between the leading citizens of Newport and their new French guests. The townspeople then gave "an illumination," with candles in the windows of many homes, to welcome their French allies.

Rochambeau, acting as much as a diplomat as a soldier, sought to ease his troops' relations with the inhabitants of Newport. He ordered that all of his troops' supplies be purchased locally. Advertisements in the region's newspapers stated that anyone with meat, eggs, fodder or other provisions required by the French army would find a ready market in Newport. Vendors were assured they would receive fair prices, paid in real silver. French troops were given strict orders to treat the Newport populace with respect. Perhaps the greatest contribution the French made to Newport was the rebuilding of the town, which had been devastated by the British occupation. French troops rented tools from the townspeople, paid for materials and repaired many of the damaged homes and buildings that the French army leased from their American hosts.

Newport residents eventually overcame their skepticism about the arrival of the French army. The Comte de Rochambeau established his headquarters at the William Vernon house, a substantial mansion; a clubhouse for his officers was constructed behind the main dwelling. The brilliant Marquis de Chastellux stayed at the Mawdsley-Bull house, and Admiral de Ternay resided at the Hunter House. There was a steady progression of balls, parties and fêtes, at which the French officer-noblemen mingled with the families of Newport's former merchant elite. The Comte de Noailles, a young French officer, boarded with the Thomas Robinson family, where he developed a great friendship with the teenaged Mary Robinson. De Noailles and Mary Robinson continued to correspond for several years after he left Newport with his regiment. De Ternay became ill in December 1780 and died at the Hunter House on Washington Street. In an extensive funeral

Right: A copper tea kettle. The Vicomte De Noailles arrived in Newport in July 1780 as lieutenant colonel of the Soissonnais Regiment, one of the four regiments under General Rochambeau. De Noailles gifted the copper tea kettle seen here, part of his camp equipment, to Mrs. Sarah Robinson as a show of gratitude for the family's hospitality. *87.1, Collection of the Newport Historical Society.*

Below: General Washington, escorted by the Comte de Rochambeau to the allied headquarters at the Vernon house on March 6, 1781. Woodcut print by Edith Ballinger Price. *FIC.2020.079, Collection of the Newport Historical Society.*

GENERAL WASHINGTON *is escorted by the* COUNT *de* ROCHAMBEAU *to the* ALLIED HEADQUARTERS *at the* VERNON HOUSE, NEWPORT, RHODE ISLAND, MARCH 6, 1781.

procession, with French troops lining the streets, his body was carried to a specially consecrated corner of Trinity's churchyard, where he was buried with Catholic rites.

In March 1781, General George Washington, the commander of the American forces, arrived in Newport to discuss strategy with his new allies. During meetings between the American general and the Comte de Rochambeau at the Vernon house, a plan was formed to march a combined Franco-American army from Rhode Island down the eastern coast of the United States—bypassing New York City—and into Virginia. The French troops left Newport in June 1781 and joined the American army in Newburgh, New York several weeks later. Washington and Rochambeau's plan, conceived at the Vernon house in Newport, eventually culminated in the surrender of the British at Yorktown on October 19, 1781, and the end of hostilities in the North. Two years later, the Treaty of Paris was signed, officially ending the American Revolution and acknowledging the independence of the United States. The war may have been over, but Newport was struggling. With little or no work available and uncontrolled inflation of both Continental and Rhode Island paper money, it was difficult to do business. Many shipping interests left Newport, and the once bustling waterfront grew quiet, as the activity in its wharves and shipyards slowed considerably.

6

LATE EIGHTEENTH CENTURY

RHODE ISLAND JOINS THE NEW NATION

Although Rhode Islanders were known for their militant independence, they nevertheless sent delegates to the Continental Congress. This powerless "league of friendship" had no executive or judicial powers and was weak enough that it did not threaten the independence of the states. Ratifying the Constitution—which repealed the Articles of Confederation and embodied much stronger, centralized power—was another matter. Rhode Island refused to take part in the Constitutional Convention of 1787 and even rejected the Constitution in a unique popular referendum held the next year. The state had too many supporters of the much maligned but successful system of paper money, or state-issued currency, whereby Rhode Islanders had been steadily retiring debt incurred during the Revolution. Members of the "Country Party," which championed the paper money scheme, were also staunchly anti-Federalist. They feared that a strong federal government would pass trade restrictions and make them abandon their vastly inflated currency. Rhode Island existed as a foreign nation until May 29, 1790, when it became the last of the original thirteen colonies to join the Union by ratifying the Constitution.

After Rhode Island adopted the Constitution, President Washington made a visit to Newport in August 1790, his third and final visit to the town. He was greeted with wild enthusiasm. Guns were fired from the fort on Goat Island to salute the new president's arrival, and ships in the harbor flew bright flags. A procession of local dignitaries and clergy waited to greet

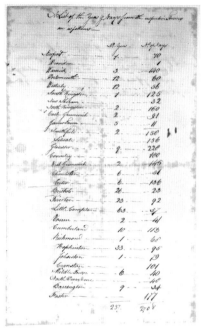

Left: Votes for and against the ratification of the Constitution in 1788, by town. Newporters voted overwhelmingly against ratification. *C#0238, Papers Relating to the Adoption of the United States Constitution, 1785–1790, folders 1–3, Rhode Island State Archives.*

Right: Rhode Island banknote, 1786. The Newport press of James Franklin may have printed this 1786 currency. *2010.21.3.2, Collection of the Newport Historical Society.*

him at the landing. Washington and his entourage were fêted and celebrated heartily during the visit. Because the devastation of war left the town of Newport too impoverished to order a set of silver or gold serving dishes for the occasion, Newport residents lent items from their own homes for a magnificent banquet at the Colony House. Those who attended drank thirteen toasts and welcomed the president with encomiums and praise.

Following Washington's triumphal visit, the warden of Touro Synagogue, Moses Seixas, wrote to the nation's leader. In the letter, Seixas noted that the Jewish population of Newport had, until recently, been deprived of the rights of full citizenship and remarked with pleasure on the new Constitution, which established freedom of religion. Washington was affected by the warden's letter. He responded that the new U.S. government gave "to bigotry no sanction, to persecution no assistance." Washington's letter to Seixas and the people of Touro Synagogue has been cited for centuries as a foundational document supporting the concept of religious freedom in the United States.

INDEPENDENCE AND DESOLATION

Following the Revolution, Newport was still one of the leading settlements of Rhode Island by charter and by law. Despite the decline in the town's population and industry, some businesses did manage to carry on. By the early 1800s, there were a handful of distilleries, as well as businesses making spermaceti candles, still operating in Newport. Many merchants returned to the business of the slave trade. When slave markets in places like South Carolina reopened after the war, ships left from Newport for transatlantic voyages to the coast of Africa, returning to sell their human cargo in the West Indies, Charleston and other southern ports. Newport merchant-mariner Christopher Fowler owned ships that transported at least 767 enslaved Africans across the Atlantic to ports in the United States and the West Indies between 1802 and 1807. In 1787, the Rhode Island General Assembly banned its residents from participating in the slave trade. However, Newporters conducted business in the trade until 1808, when a federal ban outlawed the importation of enslaved people into the United States. Some Rhode Islanders imported enslaved people illegally after the federal ban took effect.

At the same time merchants were returning to the slave trade, the free Black community in Newport was growing. As early as 1780, free Black male Newporters founded the first Black mutual aid society in the United States: the African Union Society. The organization's early members included Caesar Lyndon, Arthur Tikey, Scipio Tanner, Abraham Casey, Prince Almy, Charles Chaloner, Zingo Stevens, Lymas Keith and Abraham Easton, among others. The Free African Union Society's main goal was to support its associates in times of need. The group also worked to assist the town's Black community and to oppose slavery. In 1791, members of the society penned a document that denounced the slave trade and forbade the organization's members from associating with anyone who was economically participating in it. The Free African Union Society would later change its name to the African Humane Society. Members founded the African Benevolent Society in 1807 with the purpose of establishing a school for Black children and aiding poor members of the community. Arthur Flagg served as the African Benevolent Society's first president, and Newport Gardner served as its first schoolteacher.

Other postwar efforts to restore the economic life of Newport included the 1795 establishment of the Rhode Island Bank. Two more banks followed in 1803: the Rhode Island Union and the Newport Bank. Attempts

(16)

Be it Remembered, and it is hereby
made known to all whom it may Concern. That W
Africans, the Natives of Africa, residing in Newp
We the Committee of the African Union Society t
-ing into Consideration, thought it our indispens
duty not to Associate Ourselves, to those who are o
the African Race; that do, or hereafter be the Mean
bringing, from their Native Country, The Males
Females, Boys & Girls from Africa, into Bondage
to the hurt of themselves, and the Inhabitants of
the Country or Places where they may be brought
and sold, And that We the said Committee, for Oursel
and the Members of S.d Union Society, whom we
represent, will not directly, or indirectly, receive
any of our Acquaintances, Fathers, brothers or oth
Relations, into this Society, who is, or shall be th
Means, of bringing into Slavery, or Bondage, a
of their Nations or others, being Africans or Nati
thereof, the Natives, that are commonly called, b y
Inhabitants in Newport, Negroes, & the Inhabita
of the United States of America in general — An
also, those Members of the Union Society, who sh
refuse utterly to pay, their Proportionable Parts,
the Treasury, be discharged; and considered, as not
being Members of the said Union Society, unless
Vote or Voice of the whole Community shall de
otherwise.

Opposite: Minutes of the Free African Union Society, September 1791. This entry forbids any member from associating with anyone who derived an economic benefit from slavery or the slave trade. *Collection of the Newport Historical Society, vol. 1674B, 116.*

Left: A list of members of the African Benevolent Society, circa 1808–13, which records John Gardner, Alexander Allen and John Brammer as being impressed by the British navy. *Collection of the Newport Historical Society, vol. 1764A, 10.*

were made by the Champlin family and the firm of Gibbs and Channing to compete with Providence as the commercial hub of the state. These Newport merchants sent ships to the East Indies, which imported china, game boards, silks and jade. Others made investments in the textile industry, and eleven Newport ships were active in whaling. But none of these ventures provided lasting solutions for reversing the economic damage caused by the Revolution and its aftermath.

Newport's mercantile business was further harmed in the postwar decades by the ongoing disputes between England and France. Mariners from America were caught in the middle as belligerents from both sides attempted to cut off the shipping and trade of their rivals. Vessels from neutral countries like the United States were boarded, inspected or even seized by England and France. During the administration of President John Adams, the Quasi-War with France (1798–1800) was fought on the high seas. While some Newporters took part as privateers—armed on private vessels that were licensed by the government to attack enemy merchant ships—the maritime war brought more economic hardship to the town. This adverse environment was compounded by the threat of impressment. If an American ship were captured, its sailors, although they were U.S. citizens, were at risk of being forced to serve in an enemy's navy (i.e., "impressed").

Impressment of American seamen led to the War of 1812. Once again, Newport privateers participated, attacking British shipping for financial gain. However, by 1813, the strong presence of the British Royal Navy off the eastern coast of the United States forced American merchant and naval ships to spend months or even years in port. The privateer ships *Yankee* of Bristol and *Providence* of Newport had great success at the start of the war, but by the war's end in 1815, both ships were out of action. Newport, already at an economic disadvantage, appeared fatally stricken, with little left of the booming trade that had once dominated the seaport.

Nevertheless, Newporters took pride in Commodore Oliver Hazard Perry's heroic naval victory on Lake Erie during the War of 1812. Perry's family moved to Newport from southern Rhode Island when he was a child. His father, Christopher, was one of the first captains commissioned in the new United States Navy. Oliver served on his father's frigate, USS *General Greene*, and later commanded a gunboat off Newport. In September 1813, he marched overland with Rhode Island sailors to the shores of the Great Lakes at Erie, Pennsylvania, to help fight the decisive battle of Put-in-Bay. Oliver's younger brother, Matthew Calbraith Perry, who was born in Newport, was a leading naval figure in the 1840s and 1850s. He organized and led the American expedition to Japan in 1854 with the intent of establishing western trade. Oliver Hazard Perry is commemorated with a statue in Washington Square; a statue of Matthew Perry stands in Touro Park.

The final blow to Newport's reign as a shipping capital was marked by the Great Gale of 1815. In September 1815, waves and storm surge lashed Newport, and the winds were estimated to be the equivalent of a category 3 hurricane. Waterfront property was flooded under several feet of salt water. Homes, churches, wharves, ships and barns were destroyed on Aquidneck Island. The storm winds, laden with salt, deposited a white coating across much of the state, further damaging crops in the coming weeks. Wars, occupation, the rise of Providence as a competing mercantile center, federal suppression of the trade in enslaved persons and weather all contributed to the demise of Newport as a once-thriving seaport.

The construction of Fort Adams in the first decades of the nineteenth century was a bright spot in an otherwise bleak economic landscape. Newport Harbor and Narragansett Bay have always been safe and deep

Right: Portrait of
Commodore Oliver
Hazard Perry, depicted
as a midshipman.
*1885.1, Collection of the
Newport Historical Society.*

Below: *The Great September
Gale of 1815*, painting
by John Russell Bartlett.
*RHiX5262, Rhode Island
Historical Society.*

havens for naval as well as commercial shipping, and their defense has long been a high priority of civilians and the military alike. The first Fort Adams, located at the mouth of Newport Harbor, was commissioned by the federal government in 1799, but it was replaced around 1824 by the current fort. Part of the nation's "Third System" of coastal defenses, the new fort reflected lessons learned from the War of 1812. Work on Fort Adams commenced in 1824 and continued intermittently until 1857. Hundreds of Irish-born laborers came to Newport to demolish the old fort and construct a large and seemingly impregnable replacement. To accommodate the Irish workers, Reverend Robert Woodley, a priest from Boston, purchased a schoolhouse on Barney Street in 1828 and converted it into a Catholic chapel, thereby establishing the first Catholic church in Rhode Island.

Newport never experienced the same level of industrial expansion that occurred in other parts of Rhode Island, but it had a modest industrial base. Several steam-powered cotton mills were built, mostly on the old wharves that lined the waterfront along Thames Street. Even though these mills operated for twenty years or more, they did not become a strong factor in Newport's economy. The advent of railroads made it possible for the manufacturing cities and towns of New England states to get their products to market in Boston and New York quickly. Although a stone bridge

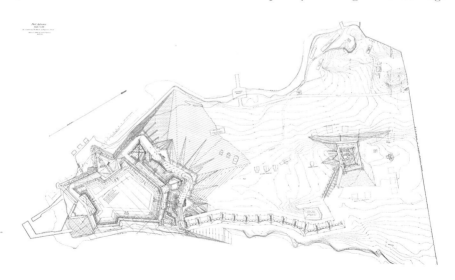

Fort Adams was built in 1799 and upgraded in 1824 to defend Newport Harbor; it was considered one of the most strategic military sites in New England. The fort was largely constructed by workers from Ireland who ended up settling in Newport. This plan of the Fort dates to 1886. *The Fort Adams Trust.*

During the antebellum period, Newport merchants George C. Munro, William J. Munro, William P. Congdon, Thomas S. Tilley, Benjamin I. Hazard and Joseph G. Stevens all lived in Georgetown, South Carolina, during the winter months, profiting from the business of slavery in the rice-producing low country of the region. Their firms supplied plantations with food, tools, supplies, shoes and clothing. The population of the Georgetown District had one of the highest concentrations of enslaved laborers in the South. *Advertisements in the* Pee Dee Times, *August 6, 1856.*

connected Portsmouth, located in the north of the island, to the mainland, it was not large enough to serve as a proper conduit for commercial traffic or for a growing network of railroad lines. The lack of large-scale industrialization on Aquidneck Island, however, did not stop Newport men from turning a profit. Newporter Benjamin Hazard successfully invested in the Peace Dale Manufacturing Company, a southern Rhode Island textile factory that specialized in producing a cheap fabric that was sold to southern plantations to clothe enslaved people.

One important result of Newport's failure to establish significant industrial development was that the streets and buildings of the town were left intact. Old houses were not demolished to make way for new factories, and elegant eighteenth-century mansions were not dismantled to provide housing for factory employees. Newport's historic townscape survived. The built environment of the town retained a charming aspect that Newport's enterprising citizens used as another sort of engine to revive the town's economy.

7

EARLY NINETEENTH CENTURY

RETURN OF VISITORS, THE HOTEL ERA AND ENTREPRENEURSHIP

Aquidneck Island, with its temperate climate, beautiful ocean views and healthful sea air was an attractive summer destination as early as the eighteenth century. After the American Revolution, Newport's many natural assets enticed a new wave of visitors to the town. In the nineteenth century, northern visitors sought Newport's salubrious climate and stunning views to escape from the increasing congestion and pollution of their industrializing cities and town. Southern visitors, principally families of slaveholding plantation owners, traveled north to escape the South's oppressive heat and dangerous fevers. The rapid increase in visitors in the pre–Civil War era greatly stimulated Newport's moribund economy.

Visitors in the eighteenth and early nineteenth centuries either stayed in boardinghouses, rented rooms in private homes or leased houses for longer stays. During the 1820s and 1830s, this pattern began to change. Spacious hotels were constructed, and real-estate speculators purchased large tracts of land that had remained in the hands of families who had received them as farm lots when the town was first laid out in 1639. The Francis Brinley house on Catherine Street had been in the Brinley family since Newport's early days. It was renamed the Bellevue Hotel and opened for business in 1825.

In 1844, entrepreneurs built two large resort hotels: the Atlantic House on Touro Street and the Ocean House on Bellevue Avenue. These luxury hotels boasted the latest in modern conveniences, sumptuous meals and

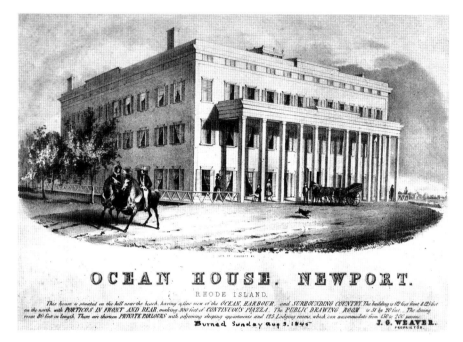

The Ocean House Hotel, built in 1841. It was destroyed by fire in 1845 and was immediately replaced by a larger and more elegant structure designed by Russell Warren. *2000.43.9, Collection of the Newport Historical Society.*

the music of renowned orchestras that entertained guests at tea parties and fancy dances. Each August, the Ocean House had a grand ball for three hundred guests. When the Ocean House was destroyed by fire in 1845, it was rebuilt in an even more luxurious style. Its wide veranda was equipped with comfortable chairs, and it boasted a 250-foot-long corridor, as well as spacious rooms with high ceilings.

Newport became known as a stylish resort for the well-to-do during "the season," with affluent guests patronizing the Ocean House and the Atlantic House. The town continued to attract summer visitors of more modest means who lodged in boardinghouses or rented rooms in private homes. This influx of summer visitors revitalized Newport's economy.

Newport became much more accessible with the advent of steam-powered vessels. Sail craft, at the mercy of wind and tide, could not provide transportation according to a schedule. Once steam-powered ships became common, regular passenger services connected Newport to other towns across Narragansett Bay, as well as the larger cities of the region. As early as 1817, the steamboat *Firefly* made the trip from Newport to Providence. Beginning with its first steamer, *Bay State*, in 1847, the Fall River Line offered overnight service from New York to Newport and Boston. It provided luxurious accommodations and dining aboard its spacious, well-appointed vessels. The line brought much-needed employment to Newport men who worked as stewards and waiters aboard its ships and who labored at its repair facility located near the docks in Newport.

The so-called "Queen of the Bay," the side-wheeler *Eolus*, carried passengers and freight between Wickford on the west side of the bay and Newport. The *Eolus* was also available for charter. The fast New Haven and Old Colony Railroad trains from New York stopped at Wickford, where fashionable visitors to Newport, with their horses, coaches and baggage, transferred to the steamer. With the emergence of steam-powered travel to the island and the construction of luxury hotels, by the middle

A postcard featuring the steamer *Commonwealth* of the Fall River Line. *FIC.2022.118, Collection of the Newport Historical Society.*

of the 1800s, Newport became known as the "Queen of Resorts."

The era of Newport's great hotels (1830–60) had a lasting effect on the city's economy and influenced its future. The opening of new hotels and businesses to accommodate visitors and summer residents resulted in the creation of many service jobs, which were filled by members of a growing Black community. The thriving economy also provided opportunities for Black-owned businesses, like the luxurious Sea-Girt House Hotel, opened by George T. Downing in 1854. Downing was an entrepreneur and leading civil rights activist who campaigned to integrate public schools in Rhode Island; he penned an "Address to Black Voters," which sought to convince Black citizens to vote against the Rhode Island governor who continually blocked integration efforts. In 1860, Downing's Sea-Girt House Hotel burned down, most likely in an act of arson by those who opposed his activism. Downing replaced the hotel with the Downing Block, a building where space was leased to fashionable shops and other establishments catering to the summer crowd. Through the efforts of Downing and other local activists, Newport schools were desegregated in 1865.

Newport's salubrious climate continued to draw wealthy plantation families from the South, who joined with the "first families" of Philadelphia, New

York, Providence and Boston. The visitors revived the eighteenth-century practice of summering in Newport. At first, these families rented private houses. Later, they vied with each other to build their own summer houses, or "cottages"—the term used in Newport for any residence, regardless of size, used only during the summer season of July and August.

The first mansion on Bellevue Avenue, Kingscote, was constructed in 1841 for Georgia plantation owner George Noble Jones. However, most summer development in the early to mid-1800s occurred on land behind the Redwood Library and along Kay Street, Catherine Street and Old Beach Road down to Easton's Pond. A new street, Bath Road (now Memorial Boulevard), was laid out to allow easy access to Easton's Beach. It was in this area that summer residents built cottages like Red Cross off Old Beach Road, designed by George M. Dexter and built for Bostonian David Sears in 1844. Southern plantation owner Ralph Izard commissioned a spacious house off Kay Street, designed around 1850 by Frederick Diaper. Belair, on Old Beach Road, was designed in 1850 by Seth C. Bradford for R. Allen Wright.

In this period, land speculators, principally Alfred Smith and his associate Joseph Bailey, altered the once-rural landscape of Newport's southern end. Smith was a native Newporter who had made a fortune as a tailor in New

Kingscote, a Gothic Revival mansion designed by Richard Upjohn and erected between 1839 and 1841 for southern plantation owner George Noble Jones, was part of the initial development of Bellevue Avenue. *P4573, Collection of the Newport Historical Society.*

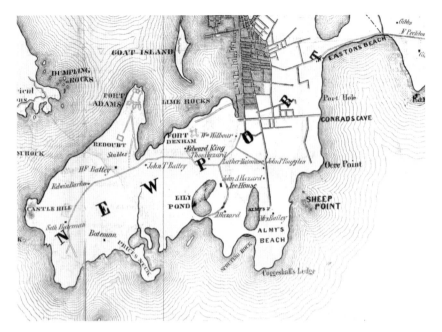

A map of Newport County (1850). Bellevue Avenue ends just past Narragansett Avenue. Between 1852 and 1853, the boulevard was extended south to reach Bailey's Beach by real estate speculator Alfred Smith and his business partner Joseph Bailey. *G3773.N4 1850.W3, Library of Congress.*

York City. He returned to Newport and, in turn, invested in real estate, doubling his original fortune in the process. Smith opened up the area behind the Redwood Library to development, and between 1852 and 1853, he laid out Bellevue Avenue south to Bailey's Beach, creating large tracts of land for subdivision and sale. This development resulted in exclusive residential areas characterized by streets lined with well-kept lawns and arched by shade trees, considered the most beautiful in New England. Many of these trees were imported specimens, and a single block, at times, contained various species of beech trees—including standard, copper, weeping and fern-leaf.

ABOLITION, ANTI-ABOLITION AND THE DORR REBELLION

In this pre–Civil War era, when visitors from the South were contributing greatly to the economic revival of Newport, two of the town's most powerful

Frederick Douglass arriving at the wharf in Newport in 1838, en route to New Bedford, Massachusetts. *From* The Life and Times of Frederick Douglass *(2nd ed., Boston: De Wolfe & Fiske Co.,1892), 16.*

political figures, Richard Kidder Randolph and Benjamin Hazard, were vocal in supporting southern slavery. Leaders in the Black community, including Isaac Rice and George Downing, and their white allies, like Sophia Little, expressed strong antislavery convictions. Rice opened his home on Thomas Street to freedom seekers fleeing enslavement in the South and to regional antislavery activists. The internationally famous lecturer Frederick Douglass, a friend of both Rice and Downing, visited Newport several times to meet with antislavery workers and to deliver addresses in support of the cause. Rice also advocated with Downing for the desegregation of Newport public schools and civil rights for Rhode Island's Black community, including the right of suffrage.

Portrait of lawyer Thomas Wilson Dorr (circa 1840–50), by an unknown artist. Dorr staged an armed rebellion against the standing Rhode Island government. *RHi X17 1558, Rhode Island Historical Society.*

Under Rhode Island's original charter, only male landowners could vote, while women and most non-white men were prohibited from voting. In 1821, people of color were explicitly banned from voting. In 1841, a suffrage movement led by Thomas Dorr established a parallel government under a new constitution. Initially, Dorr supported the idea of granting Black residents the right to vote but changed his position under pressure from a growing population of disenfranchised white immigrants. The conflict led to the threat of armed encounters between the two sides. The Dorr Rebellion (1841–42) was put down by the legal government of Rhode Island, and Dorr was imprisoned for treason. The suffrage cause, however, received a victory when the Rhode Island General Assembly met in the Colony House in Newport in September 1842 to frame a new constitution that extended voting rights to any native-born adult male.

8

LATE NINETEENTH CENTURY

THE CIVIL WAR AND THE NAVY AT NEWPORT

Newport continued to grow as a resort town during the increase in national tensions that led to the Civil War. By 1860, summer visitors, however, predominantly came from northern cities like New York, Philadelphia and Boston. Despite their long economic ties to the South and the presence of Southern families in the city, Newporters strongly opposed secession and began to prepare for the possibility of war. These political conflicts, combined with the actual outbreak of war, shattered the long-standing connection between Newport and the Southern states.

Stirring patriotic parades, fireworks and salutes by the Newport Artillery Company marked the inauguration of Abraham Lincoln, a known opponent of slavery, in 1861. The artillery company, chartered in 1741, was headquartered in a stone armory on Clarke Street, built in the Greek Revival style between 1835 and 1836 by Alexander McGregor, a Scottish immigrant stonemason who had initially come to Newport to work on Fort Adams. The company's members were staunch supporters of the Union. In April 1861, when the news came that Fort Sumter had been attacked, men of the artillery company heeded President Lincoln's call for 75,000 volunteers. Newport's quota was filled in one day. The contingent was ordered to Providence to join the First Rhode Island Regiment. On April 17, 1861, enthusiastic but tearful followers escorted the enlistees to the steamer *Perry* that would transport the men to Providence to rendezvous with other

Civil War soldiers outside the Artillery Company building on Clarke Street, date unknown. *FIC.2022.066, Collection of the Newport Historical Society.*

Rhode Island troops on their way south. Soon, the Second Rhode Island Regiment with 130 Newporters serving in Companies F and K would also be in action. In July, the regiments marched bravely into Virginia with colors flying but were routed at Bull Run.

Casualty lists were published, and the horrors of war were brought home to Newport. Thomas Harrington Jr., an immigrant from County Kerry, Ireland, who was part of the original company from Newport, was killed at the First Battle of Bull Run; Theodore Wheaton King, the nineteen-year-old son of Dr. David King Jr., was wounded at Bull Run and imprisoned in Richmond under horrific conditions. He died a few months later. Other Newport men went on to serve in a number of Rhode Island regiments during the remaining four years of the war. Lieutenant Henry Nicolai of the First Rhode Island Cavalry was killed while heroically leading his troops into battle at Kelley's Ford, Virginia, in March 1863. A baker from Newport who had been among the first company of Newport recruits to fight in the Battle of Bull Run, Nicolai had worked his way up through the ranks; after his death, he was mourned by his fellow officers, who cited his bravery and courage. A number of Newport men signed up for the navy

Right: Newport's Katherine Prescott Wormeley was a nurse and hospital administrator during the Civil War. She later founded an Industrial School for Girls on Broadway. *LOT 14043-2, no. 1050, Library of Congress.*

Below: Civil War midshipmen outside the Atlantic House Hotel on Bellevue Avenue and Pelham Street; the building served as the Naval Academy during the Civil War. *P1697, Collection of the Newport Historical Society.*

during the Civil War, including Abraham and Isaac Rice Jr., the children of civil rights leader Isaac Rice; the Rice sons enlisted in the U.S. Navy for three years in 1862.

On the homefront, Katherine Prescott Wormeley organized a local Women's Union Aid Society. Under her supervision, Newport women formed a sewing brigade to produce clothing and uniforms for Newport enlistees. She managed to obtain a government clothing contract, which provided employment for soldiers' wives and daughters. These Newport women produced some fifty thousand shirts for the Union army during the winter of 1861–62. In May 1862, Wormeley headed South to work as a nurse on Union hospital ships. The next year, the U.S. Sanitary Commission established a hospital for wounded soldiers at the former Portsmouth Grove House, a hotel in Portsmouth north of Newport. Katherine Wormeley, fresh from service with the Commission on the battlefield, was named "lady superintendent" of the Portsmouth hospital.

The Civil War had another profound effect on Newport when the U.S. Naval Academy was moved here from Annapolis, Maryland, in 1861. The Academy first occupied Fort Adams before it was moved into the Atlantic House Hotel, which faced Touro Park at Bellevue Avenue and Pelham Street. "Old Ironsides," the USS *Constitution*, was also used to house midshipmen in the harbor. Armed as a warship, the former pleasure yacht and America's Cup winner *America* was used for training the cadets. Touro Park made an excellent drilling ground. After the war, the academy returned to Annapolis; however, Newport would retain a relationship with the navy going forward.

A Post–Civil War Naval Presence

In 1869, the U.S. Naval Torpedo Station was founded on Goat Island in Newport Harbor. The Torpedo Station was equipped with a laboratory and a factory for the manufacture and testing of torpedoes and other new weapons. To further strengthen the navy's ties with the city, in 1883, Commodore Stephen Bleecker Luce established the Naval Training Station on Coasters Harbor Island. Before the training station was opened, naval recruits received no formal education or training and instead learned their trade at sea in ships. In 1884, Luce founded the Naval War College in the building that once housed the Newport Asylum for the Poor on Coasters Harbor Island.

Commodore Stephen B. Luce. Luce established the Naval Training Station on Coasters Harbor Island in 1883 and founded the Naval War College in 1884. *P162, Collection of the Newport Historical Society.*

The War College quickly became the U.S. Navy's premier institution for the study of warfare, international law, statesmanship relating to war, peace and the prevention of war. Among others, Luce invited Captain Alfred Thayer Mahan to join the faculty of the Naval War College. Mahan was a naval historian whose monumental book *The Influence of Sea Power upon History, 1660–1783* and other works were first given as lectures at the Naval War College. Mahan was an acclaimed scholar whose many published works influenced naval thought and strategy around the world.

In 1887, the first naval war games were played at the War College. This innovation, along with high academic standards, brought a new level of sophistication to professional graduate education for senior officers in the navy and other branches of the service. In addition, the War College introduced the study of international law to the navy, which soon led to the first draft code of the laws of naval warfare. The Torpedo Station, the Training Station and the Naval War College all contributed to Newport's bond with the navy and helped bolster the city's economy and prestige.

THE GILDED AGE

The real estate development that had begun in the 1850s in Newport escalated into an extraordinary building boom after the Civil War. Although the Kay–Catherine–Old Beach Road neighborhood was partially developed before the war, much of the area remained rural until the 1870s. From 1870 to 1883, more than sixty new houses were built in this part of Newport. The smaller lots on which these summer homes were constructed contrasted with parcels on southern Bellevue Avenue, where extensive grounds surrounded palatial homes. Bellevue Avenue, more than any other location, epitomized late nineteenth-century life in Newport. First laid out between 1851 and

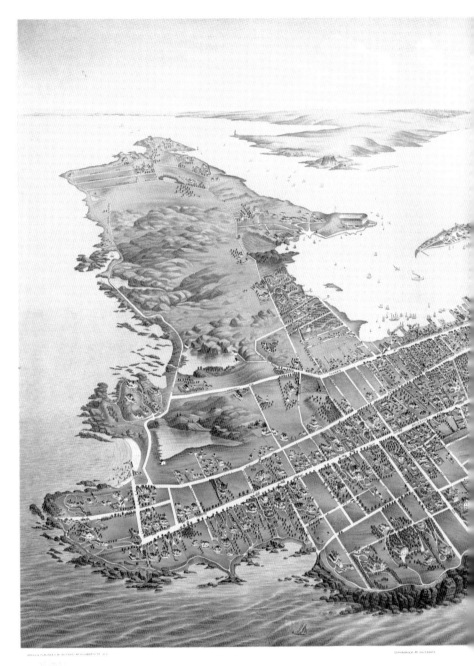

A bird's-eye view of Newport (1878) that emphasizes the summer cottages on Bellevue Avenue and Ocean Drive. *G3774.N4A3 1878.G3, Library of Congress.*

1852, the thoroughfare was famous for the grand summer cottages that were built along its length in the Gilded Age. This rapid development marked Newport's emergence in the post–Civil War era as the premier cottage resort town, more distinguished than hotel resort towns such as Saratoga Springs, New York. As the "Queen of Resorts," Newport quickly became the summer capital of the nation's high society.

Architect Richard Morris Hunt had the most significant impact on architectural style and taste in Newport during the nineteenth century. Hunt was the first American architect to graduate from the prestigious École des Beaux-Arts in Paris, the leading art academy of the nineteenth century. His first commissions in Newport were located in the Kay–Catherine–Old Beach Road neighborhood. In 1871, he designed a spacious wooden home for famed American actress Charlotte Cushman that fronted both Catherine Street and what is now Rhode Island Avenue. Also in 1871, Hunt created Linden Gate for Henry Marquand at Rhode Island Avenue and Old Beach Road. It was surrounded by spacious grounds, beautiful trees and a low brick wall. At least three other private residences were designed by Hunt in this neighborhood as were summer homes for wealthy New Yorkers on Bellevue Avenue and its environs.

The social atmosphere in Newport that was relaxed and congenial before the war shifted in the postwar period. Enormous fortunes were made at this time, and wealthy families jockeyed for social prominence. The Astors, the Vanderbilts, the Belmonts and other elite New Yorkers set their sights on Newport as a summer playground, importing friends and relatives from the rarified world of New York high society. Their summer cottages were extravagant monuments to the wealth and taste of their owners, designed as summer pavilions for the rituals of competition for social status among the families of the summer colony. Their seasonal mansions provided a sumptuous background for parties, entertainment and quests for social dominance.

The Gilded Age elite sought to appear as much like European aristocracy as possible. This new generation of summer colonists employed some of the nation's best architects to build costly summer villas in the latest

Architect Richard Morris Hunt. Carte-de-visite, circa 1860–70. *P9322, Collection of the Newport Historical Society.*

Rogers High School, then located at 95 Church Street. This architectural rendering was created by the firm George C. Mason & Son. *From the* American Architect and Building News, *May 20, 1876; FIC.2013.33, Collection of the Newport Historical Society.*

European styles. Significant New York and Boston architects who were active in Newport in this era included Richard Upjohn, Richard Morris Hunt, Henry Hobson Richardson, Stanford White and Horace Trumbauer. Many upper-class families hired the prestigious firm of McKim, Mead & White of New York to create their summer mansions. More than fifty residences in Gilded Age Newport were designed by Boston's Peabody & Stearns and its principal architect, Robert Swain Peabody. Local architects led by the prolific George Champlin Mason and his chief pupil, Dudley Newton, worked on both important and ordinary residential projects. Newport became famous for its mansions and homes that were designed by some of the most outstanding American architects of the century.

Perhaps no other summer cottage in the city quite reflected the culture and extravagant wealth of the era as The Breakers. Built for Cornelius Vanderbilt II between 1893 and 1895 to replace an earlier Breakers, the house stood as a symbol of conspicuous consumption in the Gilded Age. Designed in the Renaissance Revival style, it contained seventy rooms. The house and grounds seemed more like the castle of a great lord, surrounded by high walls and a gated entrance. Parts of ancient châteaux were shipped from France to be built into the structure. The Breakers was decorated in a sumptuous manner with expensive fabrics, art and furnishings imported from Europe. As his previous house on the site had burned down, Vanderbilt insisted that the entire framework of the building be constructed of steel and stone.

With a steady influx of visitors and residents who combined wealth with a taste for social intercourse, clubs and cultural societies multiplied. The Newport Historical Society was organized in 1853 by prominent year-round residents and was chartered the following year. The Newport Reading Room was also incorporated in 1853. A men's social club, it occupied an Italianate clubhouse on Bellevue Avenue. In 1878, James Gordon Bennett Jr., wealthy publisher of the *New York Herald*, founded a rival social club, the Newport Casino. Bennett commissioned the firm of McKim, Mead & White to design the complex of buildings still standing on Bellevue Avenue. Erected between 1879 and 1881, the Casino is an outstanding example of American Shingle style architecture. Its grass courts were the site of the first U.S. National Championships in lawn tennis, held in August 1881. Croquet was also popular at the Casino. The Newport Croquet Club was founded in the 1860s; its rule of play became the basis for one of the first official rulebooks for the sport, *Croquet: As Played by the Newport Croquet Club, By One of the Members*, published in 1865. The Casino became a cultural center for

The Breakers' southeastern façade during its construction, circa 1895. *P9455, Collection of the Newport Historical Society.*

The Newport Casino, lithograph by C. Graham. *From* Harper's Weekly, *August 28, 1880; P1892, Collection of the Newport Historical Society.*

Right: Artist William Trost Richards painting a seascape, circa 1900. *P30, Collection of the Newport Historical Society.*

Opposite: A candid snapshot of William K. Vanderbilt Jr., Harold Vanderbilt and Harry Lehr at Bailey's Beach, Newport, circa 1898. *P1714, Collection of the Newport Historical Society.*

Newport society, renowned for its summer galas, flower shows, theatrical productions and horse shows.

Newport literary folk, reformers and professors who shunned the activities of the rich had their own forms of entertainment in late nineteenth-century Newport. Author and women's suffrage activist Julia Ward Howe summered on the island, and writer Thomas Wentworth Higginson—who was the colonel of the first federally authorized Black regiment in the Civil War— moved here for several years after the war. In 1871, the Town and Country Club was started by Howe, Higginson and others as a social and intellectual diversion. Members held lively gatherings, where they heard speakers on varied topics and composed and recited humorous literary works. Samuel Clemens (Mark Twain) was once a guest of the club. Other members included distinguished historian George Bancroft and immensely popular author Fanny Fern. Famed marine painter William Trost Richards and painter John La Farge—also known for his exquisite work in stained glass— were two of a number of artists who lived in Newport during this time. Among the other important painters who visited Newport in the second

half of the nineteenth century were John Frederick Kensett, Martin Johnson Heade and Worthington Whittredge; these artists were all inspired by the topography of Aquidneck Island.

Other clubs founded in this period catered to ultrawealthy summer residents. A polo club was established in 1876. The Newport Country Club, noted for its excellent golf facilities, was formed in 1893. Whitney

Warren designed its clubhouse, which opened in 1895 on the southern tip of Aquidneck Island, just off Ocean Drive. The club was one of five charter members of the United States Golf Association (USGA). A private gentleman's fishing club, the Clambake Club of Newport on Easton's Point in Middletown, was also organized in 1895.

The Spouting Rock Beach Association, popularly known as Bailey's Beach, incorporated as a club in 1897. It was originally a part of Alfred Smith's development of Bellevue Avenue. Landowners who bought a lot from Smith received a cabana at Bailey's Beach as part of the transaction. Easton's Beach was less exclusive. It was popular with year-round residents and day visitors to Newport for its roller coaster, dance hall, carousel and other amusements.

YACHTING

Yachts of the leisure class now supplanted merchant ships in Newport Harbor. The New York Yacht Club established a summer station in Newport in the mid-nineteenth century. The club was founded by avid yachtsmen who owned impressive vessels and sponsored races and competitions. The

New York Yacht Club's Clubhouse (Station no. 6) on Sayer's Wharf, circa 1900. *Photograph, P43, Collection of the Newport Historical Society.*

club members' first cruise to Newport took place in 1844. New York Yacht Club members like John C. Stevens and William Edgar, with their impressive yachts and love of competition, built villas in Newport. Their presence attracted passionate yachtsmen from Boston, like the family of David Sears Jr., who also established summer homes in the city.

The America's Cup competition began in 1851, when members of the New York Yacht Club defeated British vessels off the coast of England; the race moved to New York and became a regular international event. The nation's first open Corinthian (amateur) regatta was held at Newport in 1874. With the arrival of the New York Yacht Club's annual regatta in 1883, Newport was thrust into the national yachting spotlight. This racing event brought yachts that sailed from New York up to Newport and then farther up the northeast coast. In 1890, after adding Newport as one of its official stops along the way, the New York Yacht Club opened Station no. 6 at the end of Sayer's Wharf. A local club, the Newport Yacht Club, was founded in 1893. Opulent steam yachts also crowded the harbor, like James Gordon Bennett Jr.'s *Namouna*, which boasted McKim, Mead & White–designed interiors and glass and mosaics crafted by Louis Comfort Tiffany.

TRAVELING TO AQUIDNECK ISLAND

During this period, the establishment of permanent navy facilities and the increasing ranks of summer visitors required better access to Aquidneck Island. While most New England communities had railroad services well before the Civil War, Newport did not have a railroad link until 1863. That year, the New Haven and Old Colony Railroad, over the objections of Fall River merchants, brought a spur line across the Sakonnet River Bridge at the northern tip of Aquidneck Island and down to Newport. The city pioneered an electric trolley system, starting service in 1889. Trolleys ran from the post office near the car barn on Commercial Wharf down Bath Road to Easton's Beach and from Two Mile Corner in Middletown to Morton Park in Newport. These trolleys soon replaced horse-drawn omnibuses in many sections of Newport. Interurban trolleys ran the length of Aquidneck Island and across the Stone Bridge to Tiverton, Rhode Island, and then on to Fall River, Massachusetts, and later, using a ferry to Bristol, the trolley ran through to Providence. At one time, it was possible to go by this "light rail" system from Newport, through Massachusetts, to Nashua, New Hampshire.

A Newport Street Railway car approaching Easton's Beach on Bath Road (now Memorial Boulevard), circa 1890. *P56, Collection of the Newport Historical Society.*

William K. Vanderbilt Jr. seated in his automobile, circa 1900. *P8766, Collection of the Newport Historical Society.*

Despite these new forms of transportation technology, it was still an impressive sight to watch wealthy Newporters drive up and down Bellevue Avenue in their perfectly equipped carriages and four-in-hands. Another mode of transportation, the bicycle, became popular during the late nineteenth century. Long, cross-country cycling trips were organized on the large-wheeled penny farthing bicycles by the league of American Wheelmen, which was organized in Newport in 1880.

Despite Newport's attachment to horse-drawn carriages, the summer colony nonetheless contributed to the early growth of the automobile industry. Electric vehicles were popular at first, and one defeated a gasoline-powered Duryea in the first automobile race in Rhode Island. A parade of nineteen electric cars took place at Oliver Hazard Perry Belmont's estate, Belcourt, which was designed and built by Richard Morris Hunt between 1891 and 1894. In 1901, William Kissam Vanderbilt, dubbed the "father of automobile racing in America," was the victor in the car races at Aquidneck Park.

LIFE IN GILDED-AGE NEWPORT

Summer residents and visitors from all social classes brought a welcome economic boost to Newport—as did a growing year-round community. At the end of the Civil War, a sizable population of formerly enslaved people arrived in Newport from Culpeper County, Virginia, and other southern locales. Even as the great summer cottages were built, Newport's hotel culture continued, and many of these establishments hosted middle-class visitors, including tourists of color. The growing resort economy encouraged the development of many businesses to support it—carting and transportation, catering and the management of the hotels themselves. The Black population who arrived in Newport both founded and found work in these establishments. As Newport's reliance on tourists and visitors grew, the opportunities for such businesses expanded. By the end of the nineteenth century, there was a thriving Black business community in Newport, with restaurants, grocery stores, banks, houses of worship and real estate concerns. Noted Black Newport residents, like Reverend Mahlon Van Horne, who headed the Union Congregational Church and served as a consul in the Virgin Islands and as a delegate from Newport in the state legislature, were city leaders.

The Allen brothers' Touro Dining Rooms at 29 Touro Street, established in 1901 by David B. Allen, James T. Allen and Henry L. Allen. The Allens were highly successful Black entrepreneurs and owned several restaurants, including the Hygeia Spa on Easton's Beach. The Touro Dining Rooms was in operation until the firm Dwyer and Purcell became its proprietors by 1909. *P1822, Collection of the Newport Historical Society.*

Irish immigrants also contributed to Newport's vitality in this era. A host of workers was needed to keep the mansions running smoothly. Many of the cooks, maids and groomsmen who lived on the estates were of Irish descent. Irish Americans also ran nurseries and floral shops to cater to the summer colonists, and some like Thomas Galvin and Michael Butler became quite prosperous. A few Irish Americans were among the Bellevue Avenue elite, including Tessie Fair Oelrichs and the "unsinkable" Margaret Tobin Brown. Oelrichs, whose Belfast-born father was one of Nevada's silver kings, used her inheritance to build her mansion Rosecliff. Brown devoted her energies to philanthropy and women's suffrage advocacy after surviving a harrowing voyage on the *Titanic*.

Some Irish American Newporters like Patrick Boyle turned to public service. Boyle was elected to the Newport City Council for the Fifth Ward in 1886 and became the city's first Irish mayor in 1895. Boyle would go on to serve sixteen one-year terms as mayor, dying in office in 1923. At the time of his death, Boyle was recognized for his attentiveness to the interests of both Newport's summer colonists and its year-round residents. Newport's close-knit Irish community, which had been growing since the first Irishmen came to the city to help build Fort Adams in the 1820s, clustered in two neighborhoods: the Fifth Ward and Kerry Hill.

Immigrants from China, Portugal (particularly the Azores), Greece, Italy, Russia, Scotland, Sweden and elsewhere settled in Newport around this time, adding to the city's diversity and bolstering its economy. The new arrivals found work in the fishing industry and in service positions for the summer colony. They established new businesses, such as barbershops, grocery stores, landscaping businesses, laundries and clothing stores.

Some year-round Newporters worked tirelessly for their community. Katherine Wormeley, who had run the Portsmouth Grove Hospital during the war, founded the Newport Charity Organization Society in 1879 to assist residents living in poverty. She started offering classes in sewing and domestic work for the poor women of the city, and in 1887, she established a girls' vocational school on Broadway that became the Townsend Industrial School. There, young women could take classes in cooking, sewing, dressmaking and household work. In 1886, Wormeley also founded an organization that was the precursor to the Visiting Nurse Service of Newport County. Thomas Higginson served on the Newport School Committee and, with George Downing and others, worked to integrate Newport's schools in the immediate aftermath of the Civil War. Mary H. Dickerson, who ran a successful dressmaking business in this period, established the Women's Newport League, an organization that worked on a broad array of issues that affected the Black community. Dickerson, a talented organizer, went on to become a leader in the national Colored Women's Club movement, spearheading state, regional and national leagues at the end of the nineteenth century.

In 1873, Newporters and summer visitors addressed the need for a local hospital to treat all inhabitants as well as sick and injured sailors. The summer colony held a number of benefits to raise money for the hospital's construction. Newport Hospital, founded by Henry Ledyard, began as a twelve-bed cottage hospital on donated land on Friendship Street. The Newport Hospital School of Nursing was established in 1886 with six female students. A new operating room was added to the hospital in 1893, and in 1903, Alice Vanderbilt donated a building to the hospital, adding thirty-four beds and the first children's ward.

The executive board of the Woman's Newport League. The league, formed around the end of the nineteenth century, worked against racial discrimination and for women's suffrage. Mary Dickerson (*back row, center*) became a national leader in the Colored Women's Club movement. *LOT 11304, Library of Congress.*

The Lime Rock Lighthouse, located just offshore, near the end of Wellington Avenue, has been the home of the Ida Lewis Yacht Club since 1928. *P9466, Collection of the Newport Historical Society.*

Left: Idawally Zoradia "Ida" Lewis was the heroic lighthouse keeper at Lime Rock at the mouth of Newport Harbor. She was a national celebrity. *FIC.2015.005, Collection of the Newport Historical Society.*

Below: In 1869, in recognition of Ida Lewis's bravery and skill, the proprietors of the Fall River Line gave her a complimentary ticket for passage from New York to Newport. *2008.6.1, Collection of the Newport Historical Society.*

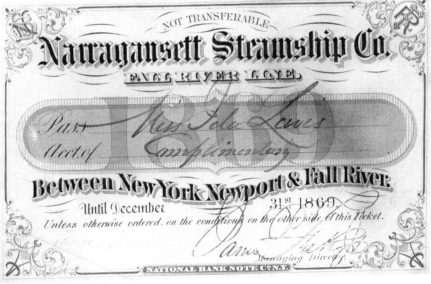

One of the most famous Newport residents in this period was Idawally Zoradia "Ida" Lewis (1842–1911). She was a Newport native and the daughter of the lighthouse keeper at Lime Rock Light at the entrance to Newport Harbor. When her father suffered a stroke, fifteen-year-old Ida took over his duties. She is reputed to have made her first rescue in 1854, when she was only twelve. Ida Lewis became nationally famous for her skill and courage in saving distressed boating passengers from the waters of Newport Harbor. Perhaps her most famous rescue occurred in March 1869, when she rowed out to save two soldiers returning to Fort Adams in a snowstorm. She was lauded for her heroism, and articles about her appeared in national publications. When President Ulysses S. Grant visited Newport in 1869, he asked to meet Ida Lewis. On July 4, 1869, Lewis was honored by a parade and a ceremony given by the people of Newport. Throngs turned out for the event. Ida Lewis was presented with an "elegant" new lifeboat. A vigorous woman in a job that was considered suitable only for men, Lewis became internationally famous and was the first woman to receive the gold Life Saving Medal of the First Class, which is awarded by the U.S. government to recognize extreme bravery.

9

EARLY TWENTIETH CENTURY

NAVY AND ARMY AT NEWPORT

In the twentieth century, Newport's ties to the U.S. Army and Navy strengthened. When the navy came to Newport after the Civil War, Fort Adams and related coastal defenses took on a new significance, providing protection for onshore naval facilities and naval operations. After the Spanish-American War, the fortifications were updated and expanded through the recommendations of the federal government's Endicott Report on coastal defense systems, first issued in 1886.

Newport men proudly served in all branches of the service in World War I. Some Newport women volunteered as nurses and ambulance drivers in France during the conflict. One Newport citizen, Dr. Harriet Rice, was awarded a medal in 1919 by the French government for her work in military hospitals during the war. On the homefront, citizens organized parades and fundraisers for the Liberty Loan program and other causes in support of the Allied troops.

A brief and somewhat bizarre event took place before the United States entered the war. A German submarine, escorted by a U.S. vessel, made a surprise visit to Newport in October 1916, causing a sensation. The German U-boat moored off Goat Island. During the three-hour visit, the U-boat's captain, Kapitänleutnant Hans Rose, paid his respects to the officers aboard USS *Birmingham*, Rear Admiral Austin M. Knight, commander of the Second Naval District, and Rear Admiral Albert

A 1918 Liberty Loan parade passes City Hall in downtown Newport. *P2519, Collection of the Newport Historical Society.*

Gleaves, commander of the destroyer force of the Atlantic Fleet. Knight and Gleaves reciprocated with an official visit aboard the German submarine before the vessel departed and submerged near the Brenton's Reef Lightship. *Newport Herald* reporters broke the story, which made national headlines. The next day, the U-boat sank five merchant vessels; three British, one Norwegian and one Dutch.

GROWTH OF YACHTING

In the first decades of the twentieth century, sailing continued to be a popular pastime among the city's elite, as well as those of every economic background who loved to sail. The Ida Lewis Yacht Club was founded at the Lime Rock Lighthouse in 1928. The Ida Lewis Yacht Club burgee consisted of a red background with a blue symbolic lighthouse and eighteen

The yacht *Aloha*, owned by Arthur Curtiss James, in Newport Harbor. Over two hundred feet long, the *Aloha* boasted a crew of thirty-eight. *P587, Collection of the Newport Historical Society.*

white stars that represented the number of lives saved by Lewis, Newport's intrepid heroine. After her death in 1911, the light was automated, and the lighthouse on Lime Rock was connected to shore by a pier.

In the twentieth century, the tiny lighthouse, now the clubhouse, was the center of an impressive number of international yachting events, such as the America's Cup Defenses, the Newport-to-Bermuda and Annapolis-to-Newport races and the World Championship of the One Ton Ocean Racers from around the world. Arthur Curtiss James was the first commodore of the Ida Lewis Yacht Club. He owned a large summer estate in Newport, named Beacon Hill House, and a magnificent yacht, the bark *Aloha II*. *Aloha II* was berthed both in New York and Newport. James cruised more than two hundred thousand miles in his earlier yachts and topped it off with an around-the-world cruise in the *Aloha II* in 1921. *Aloha II* was acquired by the U.S. Navy and served as the USS *Aloha* in World War I before it was returned at the war's conclusion.

The annual cruise of the New York Yacht Club brought many impressive yachts to the harbor, including the three *Corsairs* of J. Pierpont Morgan and his son Jack; Mrs. Marjorie Post Hutton's *Sea Cloud*; Gerald Lambert's record-breaking, tall, three-masted schooner *Atlantic*; Mrs. Emily Roebling Cadwallader's *Savarona II*; Henry Manville's *Hi-Esmaro*; John Jacob and Vincent Astor's *Nourmahal*; James Gordon Bennett's *Lysistrata*; and the luxury yachts of the Vanderbilts.

ART ASSOCIATION OF NEWPORT

Newport had always attracted visual artists, including painters, sculptors, printmakers and illustrators. In 1912, many of Newport's artists and intellectuals, among them Maud Howe Elliott and Helena and Louisa Sturtevant, established the Art Association of Newport. The association's members hoped to create a center for art classes and exhibitions in the city. In 1916, they purchased the John Noble Alsop Griswold house, designed and built by Richard Morris Hunt between 1862 and 1864 on Bellevue Avenue. The house was constructed in the so-called Stick Style, a picturesque version of European rustic architecture featuring extensive exposed wooden decoration. The Art Association's grounds on Bellevue Avenue opposite Touro Park complemented the trees and shrubs of the adjacent Redwood Library. A gallery in memory of Howard Gardiner Cushing, an artist

Richard Morris Hunt designed this landmark cottage on lower Bellevue Avenue for John Noble Alsop Griswold in 1892. It serves as the centerpiece of the campus of the Newport Art Museum. *P91, Collection of the Newport Historical Society.*

with Boston Brahmin and Newport roots and a close friend of Gertrude Vanderbilt Whitney, was designed and erected by architect William Adams Delano in 1919 and 1920.

NEW ACCESS TO NEWPORT

The twentieth century ushered in easier access to Aquidneck Island for both visitors and residents. Built in the eighteenth century, the Old Stone Bridge, running from Portsmouth to Tiverton, was the first bridge to provide access to the island from the mainland. The Mount Hope Toll Bridge between the towns of Portsmouth and Bristol was constructed during the economic boom of 1928 and opened for travel the following year. In 1931, the Short Line Bus Company linked Newport and Providence. This put an end to the Bristol Ferry and made travel to and from Newport much more convenient. However, the most direct route from New York still required two ferry rides in addition to train or automobile travel. The construction of the

A group of workers tending to streetcar lines on Broadway in the early twentieth century. *P2506, Collection of the Newport Historical Society.*

Jamestown Bridge, which opened in July 1940, reduced the trip to one ferry. The southern end of Aquidneck Island would not have easy bridge access until the completion of the Newport Bridge, connecting Jamestown and Newport, in 1969.

Newport's streetcar trolleys, which covered the length of the island and facilitated travel around the city, stopped running in 1927 and were replaced by city buses. Members of Newport's summer colony advocated against paving Bellevue Avenue, but the decision to pave it was supported by a city referendum in the early 1920s.

PROHIBITION ON THE BAY

One theme in Newport's history reemerged during the 1920s: smuggling. The Volstead Act, a federal bill passed in 1919, provided the teeth for the

A woman, possibly a temperance volunteer, detaining a man who appears to be intoxicated, circa 1920. *FIC.2022.072. Collection of the Newport Historical Society.*

Eighteenth Amendment, which banned the production, sale and use of "intoxicating liquors." As Prohibition took hold, there was money to be made in the illegal sale of alcohol. With a coastline full of small bays and inlets and a local population long used to navigating home waters in small boats, "rum runners" became heroes in Newport. Few bootleggers were apprehended, but according to local lore, some allowed themselves to be caught in order to spend the night in Newport's old jailhouse. Apparently, lacking a kitchen, the city jail would contract out to local restaurants to provide food for the inmates.

ECONOMIC DEPRESSION, BASEBALL AND THE HURRICANE OF 1938

Many Newporters lost their jobs during the financial crisis of the Great Depression. Several projects to enhance life and recreation in the city were financed through the Works Progress Administration (WPA), which provided jobs for out-of-work Newporters. One major project was the renovation of Freebody Park. WPA workers expanded its facilities to include a two-thousand-seat bleacher-style stadium and enhanced fields for football, baseball and tennis courts. Newport men also constructed a storm sewer and drainage system in the area near Forty Steps. Many smaller WPA projects included building playgrounds and sidewalks. These projects enhanced life in Newport while providing much-needed paychecks to city families.

Perhaps the most enduring WPA project during this era was the renovation of Bernardo Cardines Memorial Field. Originally called the Basin, the field was created in an area that was previously used as a drainage basin for the Old Colony Railroad; it was used for baseball beginning in 1899. Organized games were played at the field when the City Baseball League was founded in 1908. In 1937, the WPA began an extensive improvement project at the field. A stone structure was built incorporating a new set of bleachers, and a field house was constructed with dressing rooms and restroom facilities. The project also included work on drainage, water and sewer systems, grading and the construction of a new storage room.

Some of the teams that competed in the City League were from local businesses and nonprofits, like the Torpedo Station Clerks, the YMCA team, and the Old Colony Line team. The Newport Colored Giants were fielded by members of Newport's Black community. In 1920, Marcus Wheatland Jr. became the first Black man to play in Newport's famed Sunset League. Army and navy teams used the field for games during World War I. In 1936, the Basin field was dedicated in honor of Bernardo Cardines, an Italian immigrant from Newport who was killed in action in September 1918 during

The Union Athletic Club team photograph, 1934. Herbert "Tweet" Wosencroft, a multisport athlete in baseball,, basketball, and track and field, is pictured in the front row on the far left. On opening day, the team's official roster included Fred Young, William Trent, Charles Green, John Henry Wigington, Harold E. Riley, Spencer Remong, James Johnson, Arthur Greene, Ralph Williams, Clarence Butler, Frank Savoy, William Hurley and Coleman Jones. *Kerschner-Harrington collection, Collection of the Newport Historical Society.*

World War I. Aside from thrilling local games, the stadium at Cardines Field also hosted some of the top players in baseball. Especially notable were the appearances of standout Negro League players like Satchel Paige and Jim "Junior" Gilliam, who came to Newport to play games against the Newport Sunset League All-Stars.

The WPA projects of this decade helped destitute Newporters find work to support themselves and their families. However, the economic downturn in the city persisted. The Fall River Line closed in 1937; the steamship line had employed a number of Newport men either on board the steamers as waiters and stewards or as workers in the repair facility at Gravelly Point; some women had worked in the upholstery section and the main office of the line.

The hurricane of 1938 caused extensive damage in Newport and across New England. Exceedingly high winds, tidal waves and extensive rain caused flooding and damage throughout the city. Boats were ripped from

Left: The hurricane of 1938 in downtown Newport. Floodwaters overtook the Brick Market at 127 Thames Street (now the Museum of Newport History). *2019.017.012, Collection of the Newport Historical Society.*

Below: People walking through wreckage left by the hurricane of 1938 near Easton's Beach. *P4190, Collection of the Newport Historical Society.*

their moorings and docks and flung about on land and sea. Thames Street, the heart of Newport's business district, was flooded and filled with storm debris. The *Pequannock*, a steamer, was blown from the pilings where it had been secured and ended up across the harbor, demolishing five hundred feet of the Torpedo Station breakwater before coming to rest on Gould Island. The damage to homes and businesses was severe. Easton's Beach, popular with year-round residents and day visitors to Newport, endured heavy destruction in the storm. The hurricane destroyed its roller coaster, dance hall, carousel and other amusements. The pavilion, once favored for its shore dinners, sustained so much damage that it had to be demolished. After the storm subsided, WPA workers stepped in and joined Newport citizens to repair buildings, roads, docks and other structures. The hurricane of 1938 undermined Newport's well-being. However, World War II would bring a welcome surge in economic activity to the city.

WORLD WAR II

President Franklin D. Roosevelt's visit to Newport in August 1940 ushered in an era in Newport's history that transformed the city. War had already broken out in Europe, and Roosevelt sought to assess the defense capabilities of Newport, an important naval post on the Atlantic seaboard. The president, who arrived aboard the presidential yacht *Potomac*, inspected the Naval Torpedo Station on Goat Island, and reviewed 2,100 new naval recruits at the Naval Training Station on Coasters Harbor Island. Rear Admiral Edward C. Kalbfus, the head of the Naval War College, was named the chief of all U.S. Navy operations in Rhode Island.

By the time the United States entered the war after the Japanese attack on Pearl Harbor in December 1941, Newport and its naval and military facilities were buzzing with activity. In 1944, the Naval Torpedo Station on Goat Island employed some thirteen thousand civilian workers around the clock, many of them women, and over one thousand navy men and women. It was the only large industrial plant ever to operate in Newport. Torpedo operations expanded from Goat Island to several testing and research locations in the vicinity of the city. A new Naval Torpedo Station annex was opened near Coddington Point, which later became the headquarters of the navy's Central Torpedo Office, and a testing location was established on Gould Island, just off the eastern shore of Jamestown.

EXPLOSIVES DEPARTMENT, MR. HOGAN, FOREMAN IN FOREGROUND

Women working at the U.S. Naval Torpedo Station, Goat Island. *P1861, Collection of the Newport Historical Society.*

The Naval Training Station at the Newport Naval Base also saw explosive growth during the war. By November 1941, 2,800 men per month were receiving training at the station; after Pearl Harbor, over 8,000 navy recruits and draftees per month were trained there. It is estimated that between November 1943 and December 1946, some 300,000 sailors received their basic preparation for military service at the Naval Training Station in Newport. With ancillary facilities like the PT Boat Training Station and Naval Fuel Depot in Melville and the Anti-Aircraft Training Center at Price's Neck off Ocean Drive, tens of thousands of military personnel swelled the population of the City-by-the-Sea.

The rapid increase in activity related to the war necessitated a huge number of infrastructure projects in the city. Some eighty-nine structures were constructed at the antiaircraft center at Ocean Drive alone, while expansion at the naval base, including the construction of roads and housing for military personnel, opened up job opportunities. Women found work at the torpedo factory and as nurses at the naval hospital; others worked providing administrative support and meals, cleaning and other services. The electrical capacities of the naval bases were enhanced to handle the increased demand for power. A new USO club for the refreshment and entertainment of service personnel was constructed on Commercial Wharf in Newport. It was thought to be the largest USO building in the country at that time. During the war, the city bustled with defense workers, soldiers and sailors and the commercial and economic activity that came with them.

Some feared an enemy attack on Newport during the war. As World War II approached, big sixteen-inch naval guns, with ranges of twenty-six miles, were placed ashore in Little Compton, Jamestown, and at Point Judith to protect the entrance to Narragansett Bay at greater ranges. Another closely related part of the defenses of Narragansett Bay was the system of massive antisubmarine chain nets and underwater listening devices to protect from submarines. Between 1942 and 1945, German submarines sank twelve ships off the southern New England coast. While this danger existed, specially designed boats tended the nets and opened and closed the gates at the main entrance to the bay. The threat ended only on May 6, 1945, when the German submarine U-853 was sunk off Block Island after attacking local shipping near Point Judith. Coincidentally, German commanders surrendered to the Allies in Europe the following day.

During the post–World War II period, Newport returned to a time of economic uncertainty. The conclusion of World War II brought the closing of the Torpedo Station and the Naval Training Station in the early 1950s. Thousands of defense-related jobs were lost. Stone Villa, the summer mansion of James Gordon Bennett Jr. across from the Newport Casino on Bellevue Avenue, was razed to make way for a shopping center; other mansions were demolished or converted to rooming houses or apartments. The overall change in Newport's status as "Queen of Resorts" was obvious to all. The process of revitalizing Newport's economy was slow, painful and marked by wrong turns and blind alleys, but it was the efforts of Newport's residents that proved fruitful in the long run. The initiatives that were the most successful followed in a long, distinguished tradition of restoring the town's spectacular architectural heritage and finding new uses for older buildings.

10

Late Twentieth Century

The Postwar Preservation Movement in Newport

By the end of World War I, Newport was an architectural time capsule. Buildings representing every major style of American architecture, from the late seventeenth century to the postwar period, lined the streets of the city. The survival of many of these structures was due to a complex, interrelated set of circumstances. Newport never experienced catastrophic building loss from a major fire, like many cities in North America that date to the colonial period. Industrialization also bypassed Newport. With only a handful of small factories and without an intense demand for housing to accommodate an industrial workforce, many of Newport's historic buildings were spared demolition or equally destructive remodeling.

Another major factor in the town's preservation is that as early as the mid-1850s, Newport residents began working to preserve these buildings. Much of the impetus for nineteenth-century preservation efforts came from the intellectuals and architects who began to summer in Newport before the Civil War. Newporters like George Champlin Mason, his son George Jr. and Dr. David King, the first president of the Newport Historical Society, recognized the importance of saving Newport's unique architectural heritage. In 1884, the Newport Historical Society purchased and renovated the Seventh Day Baptist Meeting House (1730) on Barney Street; three years later, the Society incorporated the meetinghouse into its headquarters. Preservation efforts

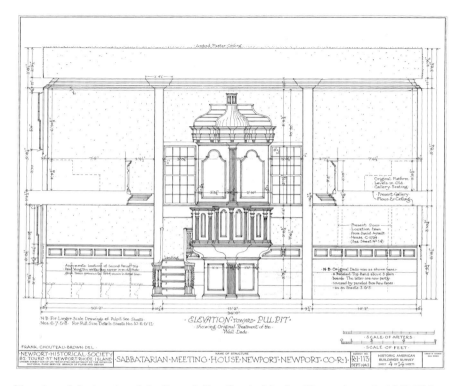

Elevation of the interior of the Seventh Day Baptist Meeting House, drawn in 1942. This documentation, gathered by the Historic American Buildings Survey, a program conducted by the U.S. Department of the Interior, has proved invaluable to preservationists. *HABS RI,3-NEWP,2-, Library of Congress.*

were taken up again by the Newport Historical Society in the late 1920s, when the society led a restoration of the Wanton-Lyman-Hazard House (1697). At the same time, initiatives to restore the Colony House (1739), Trinity Church (1725) and the Brick Market (1762) were all underway. All these projects employed the services of architect Norman Morrison Isham, whose visionary understanding of sensitive preservation helped make Newport an architectural showcase.

The next wave of interest in saving Newport's architectural treasures followed World War II. The result was one of the great successes in the history of historic preservation in America. During this period, many Newport mansions were saved through adaptive reuse initiatives. Some were converted to apartments and, later, condominiums. Others became private schools, which drew many young people to Newport. However, most of these institutions were short-lived. The exception was Salve Regina, an accredited four-year Catholic college located on Ochre Point. Salve Regina was founded in 1934, when Robert Goelet, the son of Ogden Goelet, donated his family's lavish mansion to the Bishop of Providence, who transferred the property to the Sisters of Mercy. Ochre Court had been designed in 1888 and completed in 1892 by Richard Morris Hunt. Originally, Ochre Court housed the entire college, consisting of just fifty students. By the 1960s, Salve Regina had an enrollment of over 2,800 women; it admitted men beginning in 1973. In response to its rapid growth, the college erected modern institutional structures, including a classroom building and large dormitory in the International Style during the 1960s.

In addition, Salve Regina acquired or purchased other adjacent late nineteenth-century buildings. Among those used for dormitories is the architecturally significant cottage of William Watts Sherman, designed in 1874 by Henry Hobson Richardson, who was assisted by Stanford White. Another notable Salve Regina building is Wakehurst, the former residence of James J. Van Alen. It has served as the student union for the campus. Wakehurst was based on the Elizabethan manor house Wakehurst Place, located just south of London. The plans were provided in 1883 by Charles Eamer Kempe, a famous English stained-glass artist; local Newport architect

Ochre Court, constructed in 1892 for real estate magnate Ogden Goelet, is now owned by Salve Regina University. *P10331, Collection of the Newport Historical Society.*

Dudley Newton oversaw the actual implementation of the plans until the building was completed in 1888. Salve Regina's adaptive reuse of older buildings helped preserve the historic character of the Bellevue Avenue district of Newport.

In 1945, a group of Newport residents led by Katherine Warren sought a way to save the Hunter House (1748), which was in imminent danger of being gutted. Their efforts led to the founding of the Preservation Society of Newport County the same year. Warren served as its first president and remained a guiding spirit in the organization for thirty years. In 1948, the Preservation Society opened The Breakers for public tours in collaboration with Countess Széchenyi, the former Gladys Moore Vanderbilt. The lavish mansion had been built for the countess's father, Cornelius Vanderbilt II, in 1893. Over the next several decades, the Preservation Society acquired and preserved other mansions and significant houses; among them were The Elms (1901), Marble House (1892), Chateau-sur-Mer (1852), Kingscote (1839) and Rosecliff (1902).

In the late 1960s, another grassroots preservation movement that would have far-reaching effects was launched when a group of concerned citizens formed Operation Clapboard. Spearheaded by residents of the Point and Historic Hill neighborhoods, Operation Clapboard aimed to rescue many eighteenth-century colonial and nineteenth-century Victorian buildings in their neighborhoods. The plan was to save these earlier, more modest buildings by purchasing options on mortgages as the houses went up for sale or were condemned. These options were then sold to individuals (often personally recruited by the members of Operation Clapboard) who were interested in restoring and either living in, renting out or selling the dwellings.

The success of Operation Clapboard and its offshoot organization, Oldport Association, attracted another powerful force to Newport's effort to use its past to support its future: the Newport Restoration Foundation. Chartered in 1968, the group was conceived by Doris Duke and Executive Director Francis Adams Comstock. Duke was a wealthy tobacco heiress who owned Rough Point, a mansion on Bellevue Avenue. In 1969, the Restoration Foundation acquired the Samuel Whitehorne house on Thames Street, built in the Federal style around 1811.

The Restoration Foundation's most impressive contribution lay in its efforts to rescue more modest early Newport houses that had fallen into disrepair. Through careful planning, the Foundation purchased over eighty eighteenth-century homes and restored them for rent, not for sale. The plan for the demolition and restoration of the area around Trinity Church,

The King's Arms Tavern at 6 Cross Street dates to around 1713. The building was in a dilapidated condition before its restoration by Operation Clapboard in 1973. *P5962, Collection of the Newport Historical Society.*

known as Queen Anne Square, was a joint project of the Historic Hill Committee, the Redevelopment Commission, the Newport Restoration Foundation and other groups and individuals. Through its activities, the Newport Restoration Foundation preserved nearly one hundred historic structures from possible demolition.

In the 1970s, Jamestown resident Catherine M. Wright funded the restoration of the Great Friends Meeting House (1699). The effort was led by architect Orin M. Bullock Jr. After the immensely significant building was restored, Wright presented the meetinghouse to the Newport Historical Society. During the work on the property, archaeological surveys revealed an Indigenous site beneath the northern half of the meetinghouse. These surveys and subsequent excavations in the 1990s uncovered lithics, shell pits and animal remains, all of which point to the long-term use and occupation of the site by Indigenous peoples prior to its development by Newport's Quaker community in the late seventeenth century.

After the restoration of the King's Arms Tavern by Operation Clapboard, the Newport Restoration Foundation purchased the tavern and rented it out as a private residence. *P5964, Collection of the Newport Historical Society.*

Hammersmith Farm, the one-time residence of the Auchincloss family, was the venue for the 1953 wedding reception of John F. Kennedy and Jacqueline Bouvier. *P9440, Collection of the Newport Historical Society.*

Another preserved historic treasure in the Newport area was Whitehall, the former home of Dean George Berkeley that was built on a ninety-six-acre farm in what is now Middletown, the town adjoining Newport. Shortly after he arrived in early 1729, Berkeley expanded an earlier farm structure on this site into a manor house by adding an elaborate Georgian façade. With a monumental doorcase based on a temple-front design by the Anglo-Palladian architect Inigo Jones, Whitehall represents one of the first instances of Palladian style that came into vogue in Newport with the completion of the Redwood Library by Peter Harrison in 1750. During the nineteenth century, Whitehall was unoccupied and fell into a dilapidated state. It was acquired by the National Society of Colonial Dames of America in the State of Rhode Island in 1899 and was restored during the twentieth century.

Hammersmith Farm is also a preservation success story. Hammersmith Farm was the home of John Fitzgerald Kennedy's mother-in-law, Janet Auchincloss, and her husband, Hugh D. Auchincloss Jr. It was the oldest and last remaining working farm in Newport. A nineteenth-century Shingle style residence on this land was built between 1887 and 1889 for John W. Auchincloss. The wedding reception for then–U.S. senator John F. Kennedy and Jacqueline Bouvier was held at Hammersmith Farm in 1953 following a religious ceremony at St. Mary's Church. Opened to the public in 1978 and filled with the memorabilia of the thirty-fifth U.S. president, Hammersmith Farm became a leading tourist attraction for over two decades before it was closed to tourism in 1999 when it reverted to a single-family residence.

REDEVELOPMENT IN THE HEART OF NEWPORT

Starting in the late-nineteenth century, city leaders considered proposals to revitalize Newport's harbor front and adjacent areas. However, little progress was made in deciding on a clear path forward. In the twentieth century, as the historical preservation movement was getting underway in Newport, the path to redevelopment opened. In December 1949, with federal and state funding available, the mayor of Newport appointed five community leaders to run the Redevelopment Agency of Newport (RAN). The group focused on the harbor front area, with a plan that encompassed seventy-three and a half acres bounded by Long Wharf and Touro Street to the north, School Street and (roughly) Spring Street to the east, Levin and Fair Streets to the south

An aerial view of Thames Street, circa 1974, between Mill Street to the north and Green Street to the south. The buildings along the western side of the street have been razed to make way for the construction of America's Cup Avenue. *P10199, Collection of the Newport Historical Society.*

and Newport Harbor to the west. RAN focused on traffic improvement, the restoration and rehabilitation of historic buildings and structures in the Historic Hill neighborhood, the clearance of an estimated fifteen acres of commercial and waterfront property on the west side of Thames Street and the demolition of almost nine acres of waterfront property.

One of the most radical changes was the construction of America's Cup Avenue, a broad thoroughfare along the harbor that led into Memorial Boulevard going up Historic Hill. Buildings deemed dilapidated along the wharves and harborside were demolished to make way for new hotels, restaurants, shops, offices and condominiums. Timeshare venues and hotels that prevented public access to the city's waterfront replaced structures that had stood along the harbor for centuries. The overall goal of the redevelopment of downtown Newport in this era was to transform it into a tourist center, designed to draw on the city's heritage as a colonial-era seaport.

The redevelopment of downtown Newport had its failures as well. The development and privatization of the waterfront restricted public access and threatened smaller shipyards and the fishing industry. The new, wider roadways ushered in more cars causing unforeseen traffic congestion and pollution. The gentrification of neighborhoods through restoration displaced those living in them for years, including many members of Newport's Black community.

The Newport Bridge Brings Easy Access

In 1969, visiting Newport by car became much easier when the Newport Bridge was completed. The bridge connected Newport with Jamestown and the Route 95 corridor. It also gave clearance to large naval vessels to access the naval base in Newport and the Naval Air Station at Quonset Point. A regular bus service was established to link Newport with the mainland and the University of Rhode Island. The bridge is the largest suspension bridge in New England. The Rhode Island General Assembly renamed it the Pell Bridge in 1997 to honor six-term U.S. senator Claiborne Pell of Newport, who retired that year. The new bridge stimulated the development of the city of Newport and all of Aquidneck Island.

The construction of the Claiborne Pell/Newport Bridge, circa 1968. The image, taken from the shoreline, shows the foundations of the structure and the raising of the bridge cables using cranes. *P4631, Collection of the Newport Historical Society.*

SITES OF INTEREST

Another Newport historic site that experienced restoration and adaptive reuse in the twentieth century was Fort Adams (1824). Located at the mouth of the harbor with panoramic views of both Newport Harbor and the East Passage of Narragansett Bay, the fort had been used by the U.S. Army until after World War II, when the navy took charge of the facility and its extensive grounds. In the 1950s, President Dwight Eisenhower used the commandant's house, the 1875 George Champlin Mason–designed mansion, as his summer White House. The house has since been named the Eisenhower House and functions as a venue for weddings and special events. In 1965, the State of Rhode Island took over the Fort Adams property, which still included navy housing, and established a state park on the property at-large. The Fort Adams Trust, a nonprofit organization, was founded in

This aerial view, taken around 1960, pans across the Newport Jazz Festival held at Fort Adams. *P696, Collection of the Newport Historical Society.*

1994 to maintain and support the historic buildings and grounds of this remarkable site. In the following years, the trust oversaw millions of dollars of repairs and maintenance to the buildings and property and instituted a museum and tours for visitors. In the 1980s, Sail Newport, a public sailing program, and Sail to Prevail, an organization with boats adapted for use by people with disabilities, were established on the harbor side of Fort Adams; and the folk and jazz festivals were relocated from elsewhere in Newport to the grounds of the Fort.

An additional state park was established at Brenton Point in the 1970s. Located at the southwestern tip of Aquidneck Island, the property was once the Ocean Avenue estate known as The Reef; it was commandeered by the navy during World War II for coastal defense. Brenton State Park offers one of the most spectacular views of the Atlantic Ocean on the East Coast of the United States. A monument to Portuguese explorers and navigators was erected there and dedicated in 1988. The original Portuguese Discovery Monument, designed by Charles De Almeida, was made of sandstone and was harmed by the intense weather at the site. In 2014, an expanded granite version of the original sculpture was installed. The reconstruction included a re-examination of the sculptor's original work, featuring sixteen cylindrical bollards in a semicircle to represent the points of a compass.

MUSIC: JAZZ, FOLK AND CLASSICAL FESTIVALS ARE ESTABLISHED

In 1954, the first Newport Jazz Festival took place. Originally a combination of conversations about jazz and live performances, the event quickly rose to prominence as one of the premier venues for jazz musicians in the United States. In the 1950s, jazz was somewhat avant-garde for the sensibilities of some Newporters, but the promoters of the Newport Jazz Festival persisted.

Dizzy Gillespie and his combo performing at the Newport Casino during the 1954 Newport Jazz Festival. *P5201, Collection of the Newport Historical Society.*

The performances at the festival were broadcast across the country by the Voice of America, the government's shortwave radio station. The Jazz Festival quickly became a venue for established star jazz performers as well as up-and-coming artists. It attracted thousands of people to the city.

In 1959, the first Newport Folk Festival took place as an adjunct to the Jazz Festival. The organizers soon realized that artists such as Pete Seeger, the Kingston Trio and Peter, Paul and Mary were drawing such large crowds that a separate event was established. Only a few years later, as the civil rights and antiwar movements gained momentum, folk music troubadours like Joan Baez and Bob Dylan, who appeared at the Newport Folk Festival, were immensely popular. In 1963, performers at the Folk Festival urged their young audiences to join in the March on Washington for Jobs and Freedom to advocate for the civil rights of Black Americans. The festival attracted controversy in 1965, when, for the first time ever,

Above and opposite: Joyce Wein, the wife of producer George Wein, christening the Jazz Festival stage on June 28, 1966. George Wein (*right*) and designer Russell H. Brown (*far left*) look on. *From the* Newport Daily News, *66-980, Collection of the Newport Historical Society.*

Bob Dylan accompanied his songs with an electric guitar, an affront to folk music purists.

The Newport Music Festival, founded in 1969, was an attempt by the Metropolitan Opera to establish a summer season in Newport, as the Boston Symphony had done at Tanglewood in the Berkshires. The experiment initially failed on Aquidneck Island, but the effort set the stage for using Newport's most lavish Gilded Age mansions as locales for summer classical music concerts performed by renowned musicians from all over the world. Newport Classical hosted world premieres of contemporary composers and rare discoveries of forgotten masterpieces, as well as performances of classical music favorites by both emerging and established artists.

Twentieth-Century Celebrations of the City's Past

By the two hundredth birthday of the United States of America on July 4, 1976, Rhode Island had established a program to celebrate the nation's bicentennial.

It was fitting that the preliminaries to the great Operation Sail and Naval Review in New York City on July 4 took place in Newport and Narragansett Bay. During the last week of June, Newport played host to more than twenty tall ships and a number of smaller vessels with crews from sixteen nations. Of particular interest were the two tall ships from the Soviet Union that were moored off Jamestown and later at Pier 2 in Coddington Cove. On July 1, the ships sailed out of the bay in a splendid parade heading south for Operation Sail in New York. Their week in Newport marked the city's greatest traffic jam and tourist influx, with more than four hundred thousand visitors arriving to view the ships. On the day of the departure alone, a crowd of more than one hundred thousand flanked the shoreline on both sides of Narragansett Bay's East Passage.

Crowds gather for the 1976 Tall Ships Festival, where more than twenty ships sailed into Newport Harbor to commemorate the nation's bicentennial. *2017.026.022, Collection of the Newport Historical Society.*

This bronze statue of the comte de Rochambeau stands in King's Park; it was erected in 1934 and was restored in 2019 by the Alliance Française of Newport. *Photograph courtesy of Kaela Bleho.*

Ten days later, Newport welcomed Britain's Queen Elizabeth and Prince Philip to the city before they boarded the Royal Yacht HMS *Britannia* at Pier 2 in Coddington Cove. While in the city, the queen visited historic Trinity Church and dedicated the newly created park to its west as Queen Anne Square, honoring her predecessor of the early eighteenth century who had been a patron of the church. On board HMS *Britannia*, Queen Elizabeth hosted an official dinner for President Gerald Ford and his wife, Betty. At midnight, the royal yacht, brilliantly lit and escorted by British and U.S. warships, sailed under the Newport Bridge, bound for Boston's bicentennial festivities.

Other commemorations drew tourists to Newport. In August 1978, a reenactment of the Battle of Rhode Island brought a large number of re-created historic New England military units together, including the renowned First Rhode Island Regiment. The reenactors paraded in Portsmouth and restaged the Revolutionary War battle that had taken place north of Newport and in which Black soldiers were heavily represented. The action included a mock naval battle north of Melville between Newport's *Rose* and the recently constructed Continental sloop *Providence*. The *Rose*, a replica of the eighteenth-century British frigate that patrolled the waters of Narragansett Bay in the years leading up to the American Revolution, was built in Lunenberg, Nova Scotia, by Newport resident John Millar. The sloop *Providence*, built by the Seaport '76 Foundation, was a modern, operational reproduction of the sloop *Katy*, the first ship of Rhode Island's Continental Navy and the first command of Captain John Paul Jones.

On July 13, 1980, Newport marked the two hundredth anniversary of the arrival of General Rochambeau with his French regiments. The French missile cruiser *Suffren* and frigate *Aconit* berthed at Coddington Cove. The celebrations included a reenactment of the landing in 1780 at King's Park, where a statue of General Rochambeau stands. A special commemorative postcard was issued by the U.S. Postal Service. Further bicentennial celebrations of the French presence in Newport took place the following May with the reenactment of Rochambeau's march from Newport to Yorktown, Virginia.

Observances in both Japan and the United States celebrated the centennial of Matthew Perry's voyage to Japan in 1855. Newport memorialized Perry with a Black Ships Festival, comprising two weeks of Japanese-American cultural and historical events. Every year since 1955, U.S. Navy units have visited Shimoda, where Perry successfully negotiated the Treaty of Kanagawa. In 1984, Mayor Patrick Kirby led a Newport delegation to Shimoda, a sister city of Newport, and Japanese diplomats came annually to Newport for the Black Ships Festival, culminating in a formal ceremony at the Matthew Perry statue in Touro Park. In 1985, warships of the Japanese Defense Forces with officer trainees visited Newport during this celebration. Recently, Newport Black Ships combined celebrations with events in Bristol, Rhode Island.

Mayor Sadao Suzuki of Shimoda, Japan; Councilman Henry C. Wilkinson of Newport; M. Sato, Director of Recreation and Tourism in Shimoda; and George A. Bisson, City Manager of Newport commemorating the one hundredth anniversary of the Japan–United States Centennial in Newport in April 1960. *P4691, Collection of the Newport Historical Society.*

In 1982, the United States issued a special commemorative stamp honoring Touro Synagogue, the oldest synagogue in continental North America. Trinity Church on nearby Spring Street celebrated its three hundredth anniversary in 1998, having undergone a $2.5 million major rehabilitation and the strengthening of its historic structure in 1986. As the oldest of Newport's churches in continuous use, Trinity had been the site of a special patriotic Rhode Island Independence Day service in 1975.

WORLD-CLASS SPORTING EVENTS

Golfing

In the postwar era, yachting, tennis and golfing events drew visitors to Newport from across the country and overseas. At the Newport Country Club, 1980 marked the first annual Senior Pro-Am Tournament, which has attracted many former golf champions to play one of the oldest links in the United States. The club also became a focus of national attention during the summer of 2006, when it hosted the U.S. Women's Open Golf Tournament, won by Annika Sörenstam. Prior to this important event, the club completed a major restoration of its lavish clubhouse, designed by Whitney Warren in 1894.

Tennis

The International Tennis Hall of Fame, an organization sanctioned by the United States Tennis Association as its official shrine for memorabilia and player recognition, was established at the Newport Casino in 1954. Exhibition and tournament matches were played on the grass courts there,

The clocktower and horseshoe court at the Newport Casino complex. *Photograph courtesy of the International Tennis Hall of Fame.*

and several world-class tournaments took place at the Casino each summer season. Although national championships left Newport for larger venues in New York, top world players visited and competed in other tournaments at the Casino. The Casino complex also includes one of ten court tennis facilities in the United States. Court tennis, an indoor game established in France in the fourteenth century and still played by enthusiasts today, is considered the precursor to all racquet sports.

Yachting

American yachts won every triennial America's Cup competition for over a century; the race had been held in Newport since 1930. It was as though the American vessels would never lose. In races in the summers of 1977 and 1980 the Australians won against French, Swedish and British challengers,

At the last America's Cup Race held in Newport in 1983, *Australia II* (*right*) beat *Liberty* (*left*) in the finals. It was the first time a challenger had captured the Cup since the United States challenged the British in 1851 and won. *P697, Collection of the Newport Historical Society.*

and then were defeated by the New York Yacht Club's defending entries *Courageous* in 1977 and *Freedom* in 1980.

In 1983, the unthinkable happened. Australia again beat its challengers from Britain, France, Italy and Canada in the preliminary races. The twenty-fifth America's Cup races, held in mid-September, ended on September 26 when *Australia II*, with its infamous "winged keel," bested the American defender *Liberty* in the seventh race. The Royal Perth Yacht Club claimed the Auld Mug, the America's Cup. By 1987, when the San Diego Yacht Club won back the America's Cup from Perth, Australia, Newport's chances of hosting another series of races had all but disappeared.

The loss of the America's Cup competition was a symbolic blow to sailing enthusiasts. However, sailing continued to be a vital part of Newport life. Narragansett Bay grew busier than ever with large and small sailing craft. The biennial Newport-to-Bermuda race in June brought increasing numbers of contestants in the six classes. Similarly, the Olympic sailing trials in 1988 hosted a large number of entries in Newport. One-design regattas, single-handed races, trans-Atlantic contests and 'round-the-world competitions used Newport as a starting and finishing port. In 1988, the New York Yacht Club, based in New York City, established a new summer headquarters at Harbour Court, a mansion in Newport formerly owned by the John Nicholas Brown family. Other nearby yacht clubs, such as the Conanicut Yacht Club (1892), Newport Yacht Club (1894) and Ida Lewis (1928), also participated in sailing events. Both the American Sail Training Association (ASTA), dedicated to training youth in ocean sailing, and Sail Newport, organized in 1983 to promote and administer sailing competition in Narragansett Bay, contributed to the continued strong interest in yachting. The Museum of Yachting, located in a former artillery mule barn at Fort Adams, opened in 1984 with photographs and exhibits of yachts and models famous in American yachting history. In 1986, *Shamrock V*, Sir Thomas Lipton's J-class challenger in the 1930 America's Cup races, was presented to the museum to berth year-round in Newport.

During the summers of 1989 and 1990, the restored J boats *Endeavour* and *Shamrock V* met in the first of a series of races that revived a bygone era in yacht racing. The rivalry continued in the summer of 1990 with a competition along the East Coast. In 1993, Elizabeth Meyer, John Mecray and other yacht restoration enthusiasts established the International Yacht Restoration School (IYRS) on the Newport waterfront. Using restored steam mills and electric plant buildings, IYRS inaugurated a two-year apprentice program in yacht building and restoration to help perpetuate traditional boat-building crafts. With the academic accreditation of this program, the school added further to its activities as it expanded and initiated the restoration of Arthur Curtiss James's 1885 yacht *Coronet*. One of the most elegant vessels of its time, *Coronet* is widely considered America's oldest and largest surviving wooden yacht.

A DEPARTURE AND AN ENDURING NAVY PRESENCE

Newport's long association with the United States Navy provided a reliable source of economic sustenance to the city's inhabitants through the first three-quarters of the twentieth century. Until 1973, the Newport Naval Base was homeport for more than one-quarter of the Atlantic Fleet and was the headquarters of the Cruiser Destroyer Force. In 1971, as part of the consolidation of navy operations in Norfolk, Virginia, the Nixon administration closed the Boston Navy Yard, moved the Newport destroyer fleet and closed most of the Quonset Point Naval Air Station, once the home of carriers *Wasp* and *Intrepid*. The fleet's departure was a significant blow to Newport's economic health.

Despite the departure of the fleet and the ensuing economic repercussions, the United States Navy continued to play an important role in Aquidneck Island's overall economy. Naval educational and training facilities remained at Newport. The complex that encompassed the naval base was first renamed the Naval Education and Training Center, but it later reverted to its earlier name: Naval Station, Newport.

In the first decade of the twenty-first century, Newport gained from the Defense Department's Base Realignment and Closure Program, as educational and training commands were consolidated and relocated to Newport. The budgets of these commands remained a major part of Rhode Island's economy, while the state's delegation in the U.S. Congress worked hard to ensure the U.S. Navy's continuing presence in Newport and the state.

Enrollment at the Naval War College increased with the addition of short courses, an enlarged war-gaming computer complex and growing programs for future naval leaders from around the world. In 1991, the college was accredited to award a master of arts degree in national security affairs and strategic studies. The war college expanded again in the early twenty-

The destroyer force of the Atlantic Fleet docked in Coddington Cove prior to the fleet's departure from Newport in the early 1970s. *P136, Collection of the Newport Historical Society.*

first century as its role as the navy's "think tank" increased and it took on additional responsibilities for professional military education throughout the navy. The Destroyer School, renamed the Surface Warfare School in 1975, tripled its enrollment, with more than 1,500 student officers taking courses each year. The Naval Academy Preparatory School, which enrolled more than 200 prospective midshipmen, was moved to Newport in 1974, although this addition was offset by the closing of the century-old marine barracks in 1977. Over time, PT boats, landing craft and coast guard cutters utilized the piers at the naval base.

The government's largest industrial complex in Rhode Island, the Naval Undersea Warfare Center (NUWC), the successor to the former Naval Torpedo Station on Goat Island, and the Naval Underwater Systems Center (NUSC) continued to expand. Contractors and engineers from a number of related electronic and ordnance companies established offices in Middletown and Portsmouth. In 1991, the navy consolidated the many NUSC facilities throughout the country into four regional centers, and the Newport/Middletown complex became the regional hub for New England.

Newport benefited as surplus defense sites and facilities were transferred to local communities for recreational and educational purposes and to private industry for boat- and shipbuilding. Goat Island, which formed the west side of Newport Harbor, was declared surplus in 1955 after the Naval Torpedo Station was disestablished and joined with the Underwater Systems Center. Goat Island became privately owned and developed when a convention center, a large hotel and condominiums were constructed there. The old navy piers were modernized into a large berthing area for yachts.

Rose Island, located to the north of Goat Island and previously used as a storage site for the high explosives used in torpedo manufacture, was also declared surplus. In 1969, developers who planned to construct a condominium/casino complex with an adjacent marina, purchased Rose Island. Little support for development was apparent, and there was active opposition from the Rose Island Lighthouse Foundation, a group of dedicated preservationists, as well as residents of the Point section of Newport. The Foundation was successful in obtaining a segment of Rose

During the Revolution, the British, French and American forces used Rose Island at various times. The Rose Island Lighthouse Foundation owns and operates the island's lighthouse. *P681, Collection of the Newport Historical Society.*

Island surrounding the lighthouse for development into a small park while restoration began on the century-old structure on the island, a National Historic Landmark. Later, the entire island was acquired by the City of Newport as a park and sanctuary.

In 1978, a new shipyard, Derecktor Co., leased former navy land on Coddington Cove. Three years later, it won a $350 million contract for the construction of nine medium-endurance coast guard cutters of the Bear class, possibly the largest single contract ever awarded to a Rhode Island firm. The large Raytheon plant in Portsmouth and high-tech offices in Middletown and Portsmouth industrial parks replaced dwindling industries like the GE plant on West Main Road that was built in the 1940s.

Natural Environment

In the last quarter of the twentieth century, local nonprofits in Newport and on Aquidneck Island pressured local, state and national government entities to take steps to clean up and preserve one of Newport's largest assets: its waterfront. The ecology of Narragansett Bay and its preservation for commercial and recreational sailors received increasing attention. The nonprofit Save the Bay, which was formed in 1970, campaigned vigorously for a cleaner bay. Rhode Island government officials, aware that the bay was a vital part of the state, began to pay attention to its environmental challenges and their solutions. Commercial fishermen continued to dock at Newport, but their numbers dwindled. Newport's waterfront shipyards began to close as their wharves were taken over for condominium, hotel and marina development. Friends of the Waterfront was formed to protect deeded rights-of-way to the shoreline that were being blocked or built on by adjacent developers. The Aquidneck Island Land Trust, formed in 1990, worked to preserve open space on Aquidneck Island by acquiring important sites and buying easements and development rights to at-risk properties. The Newport Tree Conservancy, another citizens group, was organized in 1987 to protect and conserve the extraordinary variety of trees in Newport. The Tree Conservancy also encouraged and assisted residents in planting and caring for trees in the city. Newport has since become a Tree City USA and is a citywide arboretum.

Weather has always been a factor in the life of Newport and Narragansett Bay. Epic storms, such as the great gale of 1815, the hurricane of 1938 and Hurricane Carol of 1954, caused unimaginable death and destruction in Newport and the rest of the state. During the latter half of the twentieth century, hurricane remnants, post-tropical gales and winter nor'easters dealt savage blows to Newport and Aquidneck Island. The Great Blizzard of 1978 shut businesses and road travel for a week. In late September 1985, the remains of Hurricane Gloria swept up the Atlantic coast, striking Narragansett Bay at a period of low tide. In August 1991, Hurricane Bob, a category 1 storm, slammed into Rhode Island. Damage throughout the state exceeded $20 million, with loss to public lands in Newport County alone valued at over $6 million, making Bob the third worst storm of the century after the hurricane of 1938 and Hurricane Carol in 1954. Two months later, "the perfect storm" added to the extensive destruction of Bob.

A potential disaster that was averted was man-made. On June 23, 1989, the year of Newport's 350th anniversary, the Greek oil tanker *World Prodigy* ran aground on Brenton Reef and over a quarter of a million gallons of home heating oil flowed into the Atlantic Ocean and Narragansett Bay off

An aerial view of the Naval War College at Coasters Harbor Island covered in snow following the blizzard of 1978. *From the* Newport Daily News, *2018.015.161, Collection of the Newport Historical Society.*

Cleanup at Hull Cove in Jamestown following an oil spill that occurred when the tanker *World Prodigy* ran aground off Aquidneck Island on June 23, 1989. *From the* Newport Daily News, *89-1116, Collection of the Newport Historical Society.*

Newport. Tides, winds and quick action by the U.S. Coast Guard fortunately contained much of the spill, and few beaches suffered significant damage.

END-OF-THE-CENTURY PLANS

During the 1990s, Newport entered a new phase of historic preservation. With most of its important historic buildings either renovated or restored, community leaders turned to Newport's landscape, streets, sidewalks and parks. The city's first comprehensive land use plan, adopted by the city council in 1991 and ratified by the state in 1995, established a rational set of ground rules to regulate commercial development, conserve open spaces and preserve the historic character of Newport's traditional neighborhoods and waterfront.

Spurred by this citywide planning effort, several groups began to tackle problems associated with preserving Newport's quality of life while still accommodating the millions of tourists who arrived each year. In 1992, the Bellevue Avenue Advisory Committee coordinated an ambitious restoration of one of America's most famous thoroughfares. In 1995, the Broadway Task

Originally called "Broad Street," bustling Broadway is lined with restaurants, shopfronts and bars. *Photograph courtesy of Matthew Lanni.*

Force was founded, dedicated to reviving Newport's historic "Main Street." In the same year, the Washington Square Advisory Commission began to address that neglected area, seeking ways to improve parking, increase pedestrian access and to highlight the square's historic character. Other groups developed ambitious plans for the waterfront area, which included rethinking the role of America's Cup Avenue and utilizing alternative modes of transportation, such as water taxis, trolleys and light rail. These planning efforts focused on issues involving parking, traffic flow, signage, lighting, safety and paving materials. Using the resources at hand, which included an informed and motivated citizenry, a cooperative city council, federal and state transportation funds, several generous charitable foundations and the resources at the Newport Historical Society, these groups laid out ambitious plans for the improvement of Newport. Despite the energy and time that went into these various initiatives in the late 1990s, few actual steps were taken to ameliorate the problems that were addressed.

Heritage Tourism and Its Challenges

In the last quarter of the twentieth century, Newport experienced extraordinary growth as an international tourist destination. Its success in preserving its historic architecture over the previous decades, the existence of a plethora of nonprofit cultural entities and its international reputation for yachting, tennis and the natural beauty of its coastline proved irresistible draws for visitors. The condominiums, timeshares, hotels and motels and waterfront changes that resulted from redevelopment in the 1970s all nourished a vibrant tourist economy.

Nevertheless, these sweeping changes brought challenges as well as rewards. The growth of tourism brought increased traffic to Newport and Aquidneck Island. Each summer, traffic clogged the streets during maritime events, concerts and tournaments. Efforts to create satellite parking lots with trolley service failed to come to fruition. The 1988 opening of the Newport Gateway Center provided additional parking spaces with a multistory garage, which was underutilized. Operated by the Newport County Visitor and Convention Bureau, the Gateway Center served as an information center and bus station. It encouraged "heritage" tourism in Newport. The Gateway Center no longer serves as an information hub for tourists; the Visitors Bureau has moved to another location in downtown Newport. Nevertheless, the Gateway Center still provides necessary services, like public parking, and serves as a terminal for the bus service. An aquarium, operated by Save the Bay, will take up some of the square footage formerly occupied by the Visitors Bureau.

While real estate development in previous years expanded the city's tax base, tourism increased costs to the taxpayers. In the last decades of the twentieth century, Newport City Councils, both Democratic and Republican, wrestled with tourist-related problems. The issues considered by the City Councils included modifications of zoning laws for short-term rentals, hotel and condominium developers, the expansion of legalized gambling in Rhode Island, pressure for more liquor licenses and finding ways to keep the waterfront available to pedestrians, boat-building and commercial fishermen. A vibrant and often rowdy nightlife posed new challenges to law enforcement and licensing and zoning decisions.

With the development of more condominiums, hotels, short-term rentals and other tourist-based businesses on the waterfront to the west of Thames Street, the city's modest industrial base slowly changed, and downtown industries closed or relocated. The city's few textile mills and electric plants were reconfigured into residences, shops, restaurants and clubs. As waterfront land became more valuable and expensive, shipyards also disappeared from the area, which eliminated support services for major regattas and any future possibilities of an America's Cup race return. However, the Newport Shipyard on Washington Street is still a working shipyard providing storage and services to the finest and most expensive yachts in Rhode Island.

11

TWENTY-FIRST CENTURY

B y the turn of the twenty-first century, Newport had become a thriving
city based on a tourist economy and undergirded by the presence of the
navy and associated businesses along with other nonprofit institutions that
enhanced the quality of life for visitors and year-round residents alike. Salve
Regina became a full-fledged university in 1991, when it began to offer
graduate degrees. Salve continued to expand in the twenty-first century
through the adaptive reuse of many of the historic buildings on its campus
and the addition of new structures. The Rodgers Recreation Center
(2000) and the Our Lady of Mercy Chapel (2010) were both designed
by postmodern architect Robert A.M. Stern. The chapel incorporated
glass windows by nineteenth-century artist John La Farge that were saved
from the Caldwell mansion on Kay Street. Another institution of higher
learning, the Community College of Rhode Island (CCRI), opened
a brand-new campus in 2005 on former navy land, offering affordable
classes and hands-on training in business, education, health services and
manufacture and trade. Additional educational institutions were added
to the area known as the North End, where Newport located a new
consolidated elementary school, the Pell School, in 2013 and the East Bay
Met School in 2014.

Some of Newport's most venerable institutions expanded and improved
during the first decades of the twenty-first century. The Newport Historical
Society (1854) and the Redwood Library (1741) built additions to their
headquarters in the early 2000s. Both projects were especially designed

The headquarters of the Newport Historical Society. Founded in 1854, the NHS has seen several expansions, with its library added in 1902 and offices added in 1915. The building was most recently updated in 2015. *Photograph courtesy of Matthew Lanni.*

Colony House. *Photograph courtesy of Shannon Hammond.*

to retain the historical features of their original structures. The Newport Historical Society expanded its programs, including a robust offering of walking tours in the historic district, and remade the Museum of Newport History at the historic Brick Market. In 2002, the Newport Public Library underwent a dynamic new renovation and expansion of its building on Spring Street.

Other historically significant cultural institutions enhanced and improved their buildings in this era. The Newport Art Museum restored and improved its campus on Bellevue Avenue. The Naval War College Museum underwent a renovation and expansion. The theater at the Stanford White–designed Newport Casino was restored in 2009 through a partnership between the International Tennis Hall of Fame and Salve Regina University; it is now the performance space for student theater productions and concerts. At the beginning of the century, the Friends of Touro Synagogue completed major renovations to preserve and modernize the historic Touro Synagogue. In 2009, the group opened the Ambassador John L. Loeb Jr. Visitors Center, a new facility for the study of Newport religious history that completed a campus composed of the synagogue, Patriot's Park, the historic Barney House and the new Loeb Visitors Center. A new museum, the Audrain Automobile Museum, opened in 2014 after an extensive renovation of the historic Audrain Building (1902) on Bellevue Avenue.

The tradition of immigrants moving to the city has continued, with newcomers adding diversity to the community and growth to the economy. In the decade before this writing, Newport welcomed residents who emigrated from the Dominican Republic, Portugal, Guatemala, Cape Verde and China.

The history of Newport recounts a story of tradition and innovation. It begins thousands of years ago when Indigenous peoples lived on the land, fished in the waters here and carved out the pathways that became city roads. The town that was Newport, founded by religious dissenters from Puritan orthodoxy and people of varied faiths, became a lively and thriving seaport in the eighteenth century. Yet the town's very success as a center of commerce derived from the enslavement of Africans who were captured and brought to Newport unwillingly. In the ensuing centuries, Newport underwent several periods of economic malaise and distress, but enterprising inhabitants eventually found ways to bring it back to health. Its salubrious climate and stunning landscape have always been its glory, and the people who make up its population, descended from a wide assortment of countries and locales, are its greatest assets. As Newport forges ahead into the twenty-first century, the road forward will not be easy, but if the past is any indication, Newport will continue to thrive, as it strives to balance the challenges of a city committed to history and tourism with those of a city equally concerned with the health and happiness of its permanent year-round residents.

About the
Newport Historical Society

The Newport Historical Society (NHS) was founded in 1854. Its purpose is to collect, document and preserve Newport's unique contribution to the national narrative over the course of five centuries. The continuing mission of the NHS is to chronicle, advocate for and communicate this history to a broad audience so that knowledge of our past will contribute to a deeper understanding of the present and better preparation for the future. The Newport Historical Society retains and preserves artifacts and documents and is the steward of six historic properties.